# BUDDHISM FOR BEGINNERS

Learn How to Put the Teachings Into Practice to Find Your Peace

(A Guide to the Fundamental Beliefs and Traditions of Buddhism)

Rebecca Lawson

Published by Andrew Zen

**Rebecca Lawson**

All Rights Reserved

*Buddhism for Beginners: Learn How to Put the Teachings Into Practice to Find Your Peace (A Guide to the Fundamental Beliefs and Traditions of Buddhism)*

ISBN 978-1-77485-160-9

All rights reserved. No part of this guide may be reproduced in any form without permission in writing from the publisher except in the case of brief quotations embodied in critical articles or reviews.

Legal & Disclaimer

The information contained in this book is not designed to replace or take the place of any form of medicine or professional medical advice. The information in this book has been provided for educational and entertainment purposes only.

The information contained in this book has been compiled from sources deemed reliable, and it is accurate to the best of the Author's knowledge; however, the Author cannot guarantee its accuracy and validity and cannot be held liable for any errors or omissions. Changes are periodically made to this book. You must consult your doctor or get professional medical advice before using any of the suggested remedies, techniques, or information in this book.

Upon using the information contained in this book, you agree to hold harmless the Author from and against any damages, costs, and expenses, including any legal fees potentially resulting from the application of any of the information provided by this guide. This disclaimer applies to any damages or injury caused by the use and application, whether directly or indirectly, of any advice or information presented, whether for breach of contract, tort, negligence, personal injury, criminal intent, or under any other cause of action.

You agree to accept all risks of using the information presented inside this book. You need to consult a professional medical practitioner in order to ensure you are both able and healthy enough to participate in this program.

# Table of Contents

INTRODUCTION .................................................................... 1

CHAPTER 1: THE TEACHINGS OF BUDDHA ......................... 3

CHAPTER 2: BASICS OF BUDDHISM: TRADITIONS AND BELIEFS .................................................................................. 18

CHAPTER 3: LOOK! THE JEWEL IN THE LOTUS! ................. 30

CHAPTER 4: DIFFERENT SCHOOLS OF BUDDHISM ............ 39

CHAPTER 5: THE NATURE AND DZTULE OF THE BUDDHA'DZ TEASHING ............................................................................. 47

CHAPTER 6: THE TEACHINGS OF BUDDHISM..................... 49

CHAPTER 7: DIFFERENT BUDDHIST TRADITIONS AND HOW WE ACT ON OUR PRACTICE ................................................ 59

CHAPTER 8: APPROACHING THE STUDY............................ 67

CHAPTER 9: BUDDHIST TEACHINGS ................................... 70

CHAPTER 10: NIRVANA - WHAT IS IT AND WHY IS IT IMPORTANT IN BUDDHISM ................................................ 77

CHAPTER 11: MEDITATION AS AN INTEGRAL PART OF BUDDHISM........................................................................... 93

CHAPTER 12: HOW DID BUDDHISM ORIGINATE?............. 96

CHAPTER 13: THE RULES OF KARMA............................... 103

CHAPTER 14: BUDDHIST TEMPLES .................................. 117

CHAPTER 15: TOLERANCE................................................. 128

CHAPTER 16: THE FUNDAMENTAL BELIEFS OF BUDDHISM ................................................................................. 132

CHAPTER 17: DIFFERENT SCHOOLS OF BUDDHISM ........ 138

CHAPTER 18: PRECEPT OF RIGHT SPEECH ...................... 162

CHAPTER 19: THE BUDDHIST SEARCH FOR AFTERLIFE.... 168

CHAPTER 20: MEDITATION PREPARATION ..................... 176

CHAPTER 21: IS IT A RELIGION OR PHILOSOPHY? .......... 181

CONCLUSION .................................................................. 183

# Introduction

Many people mistake Buddhism for an ancient religion. It is a religion that is not relevant to our modern society and is mystical, and is only practiced by a handful of people in India. Although this religion was founded in India, many of its teachings can be applied to everyday life.

This guidebook will look at a few basic aspects of Buddhism. It will also try to connect them to your current life. Many people feel that something is missing. They are constantly looking for more. Even if you don't think of the Four Noble Truths as Buddhist religion, these feelings can be correlated to the Four Noble Truths. We will discuss the Four Noble Truths within the context of our daily lives and then we'll also talk about each of the Eightfold Paths and what they tell us to live a happy and healthy life.

The guidebook will begin with an introduction to Buddhism, including how it began, its growth, and the basic truths and tenets. After that, we will move on to discuss the Four Noble Truths and the Eightfold Path. We will then relate these ideas to your everyday life and help you to overcome any dissatisfaction you may have had in the past.

Finally, we'll spend the last part of the guidebook discussing how to overcome cravings and other impermanent issues in your life. Although it isn't going to be easy you can draw on some of the wonderful features of Buddhism to help you along your journey.

Although some may believe Buddhism is dead and no longer relevant, it is a religion that draws on the same ideas as other religions. It is important to be kind to people and to understand how to control your thoughts and actions. You should also learn to protect others. Although the final goal might be different than what you believe in, it is certain that these truths will be of great help to you. This guidebook will help you learn how Buddhism can improve your life.

# Chapter 1: The Teachings of Buddha

The Buddha saw the human race in a lotus flower bed shortly after his Enlightenment. Some lotuses were still stuck in the mud while others were emerging from the mud and some others were at the brink of blooming. All people were capable of achieving their full potential, and all needed a little assistance. The Buddha chose to teach and all the teachings of Buddhism could be considered attempts to realize this vision, to help people move towards Enlightenment.

Buddhism views life as a constant process of change and its practices seek to capitalize on this fact. This means that you can make positive changes in your life. Mindfulness is the key to changing your mind. Buddhism offers many ways to work on this. Meditation is the most important practice of Buddhists. It helps to develop more positive states of mind, such as calm, concentration and awareness. Meditation can help you gain a deeper understanding of yourself, others, and life. Buddhists don't seek to 'evangelise or coerce' others to follow their religion. However, they do want to make the teachings of Buddhism available to anyone who is interested. People are free to take as many or as few as they wish.

These ideals are collectively called the 'Three Jewels, or the Three Treasures'. These are the Buddha (the yellow gem), the Dharma, the blue jewel, and the Sangha(the red jewel). These are the three central principles that will guide your life and make you a Buddhist.

The Buddha

The historical Buddha, as well as the ideal of Buddhahood, is called the Buddha. All schools of Buddhism consider the historical Buddha their inspiration, founder, and guide. To seek refuge to the Buddha is to see him as your spiritual teacher and example. This also means you are committing to Buddhahood, which is

Enlightenment of all beings. It means you want to be someone who sees reality as it really is and lives in harmony with that vision. This is the ultimate goal of the Buddhist spirituality, which represents the end of all suffering.

The Dharma

The Dharma refers to the teachings of Buddha or the truth that he understood. Although there are many meanings to the word "Dharma", the most important is that it refers to the unmediated Truth, as experienced by an enlightened mind. It also includes Buddhist teachings, which are the same Truth that is mediated through language and concepts. Dharma, in this second sense, refers to the teaching that Buddha first expressed his realization in words and then communicated it to others at Sarnath (North India). This event is commonly known as the "first turning of the Dharma wheel", and the eight-spoked Dharma wheels are a common symbol of Buddhism.

Dharma is also a term that refers to all scriptures considered to be part of the Buddhistcanon. These include the Pali Canon, which records the life of Buddha, as well as later scriptures and written teachings of people who have reached Enlightenment through the centuries. It is a vast literature with unparalleled riches, and the entire canon is more than 100 times longer than the Bible. It includes works like The Dhammapada and The Diamond Sutra.

Dharma can also refer to the practices described in the scriptures. The essence of Buddhism, despite the vast amount of literature available, is simple: It is about finding ways to transform yourself. According to The Dhammapada, it can be summarized as "learning to do good; ceasing doing evil; purifying one's heart".

The Dharma is a refuge. This means that you should see these teachings as the most accurate guide to reality and commit to practicing them. Triratna emphasizes the central teachings common to all main schools. These teachings encourage mindfulness and kindness and help us to see how our thoughts affect our lives.

The Buddha's main teachings will be explored and connected with the great Buddhist qualities wisdom and compassion. Engaging in basic Buddhist practices is a way to understand and engage with deeper teachings of Buddhism. Sangharakshita says, 'There are not higher teachings, but only deeper realizations.

Our radical approach is in the sense that we return to the animating spirit as well as the foundational teachings. Any part of this tradition can serve as an inspiration, provided it is an expression or the Dharma. People can now be called heirs of the entire Buddhist tradition, an incomparable source of spiritual experience and guidance.

The Sangha

We all need to be taught by others. We need to learn from others who have practiced the Dharma, particularly those who have insight into the nature and meaning of reality. The third of the three Jewels, or the spiritual community, is the Sangha.

"Sangha" also refers more broadly to those with whom we share our spiritual lives. The guidance and friendship of others who are further along the path is crucial. This is vital because Buddhism isn't an abstract philosophy or creed. It is a way to approach life, and it can only be understood when it is lived in others. In the broadest sense, the Sangha refers to all the Buddhists around the world and all the ones of the past or future.

The ideals of Buddhism are also represented in the archetypal Bodhisattvas, who are archetypal figures. Avalokitesvara, for example, is the embodiment and embodiment of Compassion. He is shown with four, eight or a thousand arms that he uses to help all living creatures. Manjusri, the embodiment and embodiment of Wisdom, is depicted holding a sword that he uses to cut through ignorance. The third of the Three Jewels, which is the Sangha, or the spiritual community, is composed of the Bodhisattvas together with the other Enlightened teachers.

"Sangha" also refers more broadly to those with whom we share our spiritual lives. The guidance and friendship of others who are further along the path is crucial. This is vital because Buddhism isn't an abstract philosophy or creed. It is a way to approach life, and it can only be understood when it is lived in others. In the broadest sense, the Sangha refers to all the Buddhists around the world and all the ones of the past or future.

The ideals of Buddhism are also represented in the archetypal Bodhisattvas, who are archetypal figures. Avalokitesvara, for example, is depicted as the embodiment and embodiment of Compassion. He is shown with four, eight or a thousand arms that he uses to help all living creatures. Manjusri, the embodiment and embodiment of Wisdom, is shown carrying a sword that he uses to cut through ignorance. The Arya Sangha, or community of the Noble Ones, is a group that includes the Bodhisattvas as well as other enlightened teachers.

Our Sangha

Kalyana mitrata, or spiritual friendship or 'friendship to what is beautiful' as it was known by Buddha, is the entirety of the spiritual life. These words are what our community takes to heart. Kalyana mitrata could be described as the entire Triratna Buddhist Community. Triratna centres do more than teach meditation techniques or provide information about Buddhism. A person is considered a friend when they first visit a Triratna center. They can participate in all activities at the centre, such as meditation classes, Buddhist study and practice, and arts events. They are not required to become more involved, but some Friends remain Friends for many years. There are many opportunities to meet other practitioners and to strengthen existing relationships. All of the structures in the community can be seen as a platform for friendship and kalyana mitrata.

The Triratna Buddhist Order is at the heart of the Triratna Buddhist community. The Order is not monastic nor lay; some members of the Order have families while others are celibate anagarikas. Some may live in Triratna's residential communities or team-based work situations. It can be very beneficial to share your life or work with other Buddhists. It is not about the lifestyle that Order members choose to live, but the spiritual commitment they have made. They share their spiritual lives and work together to spread the Dharma. Any man or woman, regardless of race, gender, class, gender or sexuality, can join the Order if they are truly and effectively committed to practicing the Dharma.

The Threefold Way of Ethics, Meditation, and Wisdom is another way to describe the path. This is a progressive route, since ethics and a clear conscience are essential for meditation. Meditation is the foundation on which wisdom can grow.

## Ethics

Living is to act. Our actions can have both harmful and beneficial effects on ourselves and others. Buddhist ethics is concerned about the principles and practices that encourage one to act in a way that helps rather than harm.

The core ethical code is known as the Five Precepts. These are not rules or commands, but rather 'principles for training' that can be freely applied with intelligence and sensitivity. Buddhist tradition recognizes the complexity of life and all its difficulties. It does not suggest there is one right way to do things. Buddhism does not speak of actions being wrong or right. Instead, it speaks of them as skillful (kusala), or unskillful (akusala). Many Buddhists across the globe recite these five sentences.

Every day, practice the following principles.

## Wisdom

All Buddhist practices, including meditation and meditation, aim to attain prajna or wisdom. Buddha taught us that our fundamental cause for human problems is our existential ignorance. We fail to see the true nature and value of reality. Wisdom is the opposite. We need to first hear the Buddhist vision of the life. Next, we must reflect upon them and apply them to our own lives. Prajna is the actual process of discovering the truth.

It doesn't suffice to be able to understand the Buddha's philosophy. Realizing the truth is the ultimate goal and being transformed by it is the ultimate goal.

Buddha taught that all of life, including everything we experience, has three characteristics. These are the three characteristics of conditioned existence, he said. He stated that all life was dukkha, which means unsatisfactory. It is also impermanent, he said. Everything in the universe, including us and our thoughts, is constantly changing. Yet, we believe that the world around us can be predicted and controlled. We live our lives as though death is not possible. Buddhists contemplate the reality of impermanence and strive to live with it. Thirdly, although we might look for stability and permanence in our lives, we find only change. He said that all of existence is either anatta or insubstantial. There is no fixed, abiding essence or eternal soul in things.

Being wise in Buddhist terms will see the world in these marks or qualities. Prajna is the ability to let go of the pleasant illusions we make to make our lives easier and to live more in accordance with these truths. The ability to understand that nothing lasts or has any fixed substance has a transformative effect. This means that all things in life are interconnected. No one is completely separate from others, and humanity is not isolated from the world around it. This naturally leads to compassion, which is universal loving-kindness. It is also the counterpart to wisdom.

Perhaps the most fundamental form of Buddha's teaching is the Four Aryan Truths (or Noble Truths). These truths are as follows:

1. Dukkha is the basis of all existence. The word dukkha has been variously translated as 'suffering', 'anguish', 'pain', or 'unsatisfactoriness'. Buddha realized that life is a struggle and that we don't find happiness or satisfaction in everything we experience. This is the problem with existence.

2. Dukkha is caused by craving. Our natural tendency as humans is to blame external factors for our problems. The Buddha says their root is in the mind. Particularly, our tendencies to grab at things or push them away puts us at odds with how life is really.

3. With the end of dukkha, comes the end of craving. We are the cause of all our problems, but we can also solve them.

While we cannot control the events that occur to us, we can alter our responses.

4. From dukkha, there is a way. The Buddha does not take responsibility for the actions of others, but he did teach methods that can help us change our behavior, such as the Noble Eightfold Path.

The Buddha's "Noble Eightfold Path" is an additional 'unpacking of the Threefold Way'. It is probably the most well-known of all the Buddha's teachings. It dates back to the Buddha's first discourse. It is an ancient teaching that is highly valued for its wisdom and practical guidance. The teaching was traditionally viewed as highlighting eight areas of right practice (Sangharakshita preferred 'perfect' to "right"), which are in mutual relation and essential components in an integrated approach towards the Dharma.

Perfection Vision or Right Understanding

Right Resolution or Perfect Emotion

Perfect speech or right speech

Correct Action or Perfect Action

Right Life or Perfect Living

Right effort or perfect effort

Right Mindfulness, or Perfect Awareness

Right Meditation or Perfect Samadhi

## Chapter 2: Basics of Buddhism: Traditions and Beliefs

This chapter will help you get a better understanding of Buddhism. It is important not to let its complexity scare you. Learning about Buddhism can be very rewarding. It is a way to live and a religion that has been adopted by nearly 300 million people. It is a way of life that explains the injustices and inequalities in the world and helps followers to deal with them. Siddhartha Gautama is often seen as a role model. It is through his teachings that Buddhists can find the path to enlightenment. Siddhartha Gautama was born to a royal family. He realized that luxury and wealth don't guarantee happiness. Siddhartha spent six years exploring various teachings, philosophy, and religions in his quest to find the secret to happiness. He was able to attain enlightenment and dedicate his life to sharing the principles of Buddhism with others. The Buddha was not a God, and never claimed to have been one. His experiences were used to show a specific path to enlightenment but he never claimed divinity.

Buddha's teachings began with the realization that wealth doesn't guarantee happiness. Learning about Buddhism can help you find true happiness, no matter how rich or poor you may be. This will be a powerful message for many people, since many people live with a lackluster life and feel empty. We define success as having wealth or possessions. Buddhism teaches you that happiness is not limited to material wealth. It is possible to discover that wealth is only a part of a greater whole.

Buddhism has developed into many different sects and is subject to cultural interpretations. However, Buddhism is open to all religions and beliefs.

Understanding and recognizing the fundamental precepts of Buddhism is essential in order to understand it. These are the essential elements of Buddhism's beliefs, practices, and traditions. Here is a summary of key elements of Buddhism.

The Three Jewels

*   The historical Buddha and Buddhahood: Also known as the Buddha. The whole tradition is derived from Buddha, and Buddhists regard him as their guide, inspiration, and founder. Individuals who seek refuge in Buddha are able to see him as their ultimate teacher and spiritual model. It's also about becoming a Buddha, and living in accordance to that vision.

*   The Dharma is the mind and teachings of Buddha. It also includes the truth he discovered through his life and experiences. Buddha put his realizations into words and shared them with others to create the Dharma.

*   The Sangha is what we refer as a person's spiritual group. You will need to have people to learn from in order to fully grasp the Buddhist teachings. This includes the teachings and examples of others who have gone before you. It is a group of

people who share the same spiritual life, and most of them are further along the path. This is important because Buddhism is seen as a way of life, and can only be meaningful when it is shared and grown.

## The Noble Truths

The four noble truths are another fundamental part of Buddhism. These truths emphasize suffering, not in an attempt to portray the world as bad but with the intent of explaining it as it is. You will eventually realize that sickness, aging and death are inevitable. These four noble truths are summarized as follows:

\*      Dukkha – Suffering is real and it exists.

\*      Samudaya – There is a reason for every suffering

\*      Nirodha – There is an end for all suffering.

\*      Magga – To end suffering one must follow the Eightfold Path.

## The Eightfold Path

The noble Eightfold Path is the last of the four noble truths. This path, exactly as Siddhartha Gatama described it, explains the way a person can end their suffering. This guideline will serve as a practical guideline for moral and mental development. These are:

* Right view
* Right intention
* Right speech
* Right action
* Right livelihood
* Right effort
* Right mindfulness
* Concentration is key

The Buddhist Precepts

Buddhists must observe the Buddhist precepts. They help cultivate mindfulness and truthfulness. According to Buddhists, if they follow at least five precepts, it is believed that they will grow spiritually and morally. These are the precepts:

5 Precepts

* Avoid killing living things
* Avoid stealing
* Refrain from sexual misconduct
* Refrain From Lying
* Avoid intoxicants

8 Precepts

* Avoid eating at unsuitable times
* Refrain from performing, singing, dancing or playing music.
* Avoid using perfumes, cosmetics and garland

10 Precepts

* Avoid high-heeled chairs and sleep on luxurious, soft beds.
* Refrain from accepting any money

The Five Skandhas

The five aggregates, which are believed to exist within the mind and body, will also be mentioned. They do not exist in isolation from the body and they cannot exist without the body. The fact that you have a mind and a body means that you already possess the Buddha nature and the five aggregates. This is how Buddhism teaches that you can attain all that Buddhism has to offer.

* Rupa - matter.

* Vinnana - consciousness.

* Vedana - feeling.

* Sanna – perception and memory.

* Sankhara - Mental formations

After you have learned the basics, I'm sure that you can pick up some lessons. You don't need to learn all the teachings that can positively affect your life. Our goal is not to convert but to live in harmony with the Buddhist way and learn how to transform ourselves.

TRADITIONS & BELIEFS

Buddhism, like many other religions and ways of living, isn't one system of beliefs or thoughts. It's a collection. Because Buddha's teachings were different, there were splits and distinct practices that developed after Buddha Gautama died. Three main schools emerged as the dominant ones: Vajrayana, Mahayana and Theravada.

Theravada Buddhism

Theravada Buddhism is also known as Southern Buddhism. It has approximately 100 million followers. This religion was first established in Sri Lanka by Buddhist missionaries from India. It spread to Laos and Burma, Thailand as well as Cambodia, Laos, Burma and Thailand later. This led to Separative teaching or the Vibhajjavada school. Theravada Buddhism was already well-established in other parts of the world by the end of the 15th century. Some examples of these practices are:

\*      Dana - A thoughtful and ceremonial gift.

* Karma - Balances accumulated merit and sin, and helps to determine one's fate in the future.

* Sila - Learning Buddhist lessons and putting them into practice. You can add 3 teachings to special days that include entertainment and comfort, as well as restricting ornamentation.

* Paritta - Ritual chanting.

* Festivals - These are the three days during which the full moon and the lunar cycle are celebrated. The agricultural year is tied to many celebrations and festivals.

* Worship - Items made by Buddha, relics Buddha and other symbolic items.

* The cosmos — Explains the many levels of the universe, including 21 heavenly realms as well as four underworlds. The worlds of billions of people are combined into clusters. They then merge into galaxies and are then combined into super-galaxies.

\* Pilgrimages – Mostly found at Buddhist sites in India or Sri Lanka.

## Mahayana Buddhism

Mahayana Buddhism, also known as Northern Buddhism in Korea, Japan and China, is the dominant religion of Korea, Japan, China and a part of Vietnam. Between 206 BCE to 220 CE, the tradition reached China and was accepted by the poor. Later, it gained acceptance and popularity among the ruling class. It reached Japan in the 6th century. Many schools were established (e.g. meditation school, Pure Land teachings, Huayen and T'ein Tai). They celebrate harvest festivals and New Year.

## Vajrayana Buddhism

Tantric Buddhism is a religion with approximately ten million followers across Tibet, China and Russia. The Padmasambhava brought it to Tibet in response to the King's request. However, there was conflict between Buddhism and Bon, the native Tibetan religion. The religion was revived by the Dalai Lama in the 11th century CE, as he was the head the Gelu school for Buddhist teachings. It is important to emphasize ritual and ceremony. Later, the practice of finding a young child to replace the principal teacher was established. They celebrate harvest festivals, New Years and five anniversaries that mark important events in Buddha's life. The Cultural Revolution in China saw the Tibetan and Buddhist societies suffer greatly when all religious beliefs were attempted to be eradicated.

Principal Practices

Buddhism has evolved over time to fit in with different cultures. It is important to remember that the practices of Buddhism are constantly changing. However, it is important to describe some of the more traditional Buddhist practices. These practices are focused on seeking karmic benefits by helping others, and avoiding future karmic retribution. You can also use rituals and practices to focus your mind and purify it. These are:

*       Prayers - There are many ways to pray. It is a good idea to test each one to see which one works best for you and how it helps you to understand yourself better.

*       Chanting - This sound is common among Buddhists, who believe that chanting can protect them. They chant when they sense danger or during significant life events.

*       Meditation - It is a fundamental practice of Buddhism. Because it is often the only way to attain enlightenment, meditation is often a key component. Meditation is important for its many benefits to mental and physical health. Meditation improves mental abilities, relaxation, happiness, and overall well-being.

*       Vegetarianism: Although the Buddha didn't prohibit people from eating meat or vegetables, many Buddhists are vegetarians.

## Chapter 3: Look! The Jewel In The Lotus!

This is the classic Buddhist chant. The "mani", also known as the mantra, is believed to be a powerful tool for generating compassion. The mantra can also be a powerful practice that can bring joy and peace to the person who recites it.

Although the Sanskrit words "om padme huum" translate as English words that form the title of the chapter, their meaning is infinitely more. The mantra, which is a reminder of the lotus flower, a sacred symbol for Buddhism, invites people to speak six syllables and see the Nirvana's best fruit, which is embodied in this sacred flower.

The lotus flower is an emblem of rebirth, and the blossoming of enlightenment. The lotus is a flower that grows in the mud. It emerges from the water and blossoms into a multitude of petals. The lotus is a symbol for humanity's ability and will to transcend the illusions of the world, and achieve enlightenment. Humans are humble in origin and seek the light that dances on the surface water. The human soul is like the lotus. It grows towards the gathering light. The flower begins to blossom when it is still in its bud. The lotus blossoms into its best self when it is exposed to the sunlight. The human being can attain enlightenment. Although the journey to the light is difficult, the goal is the realization of all its potential and the blessing of the world with beauty.

The jewel of enlightenment is at the center of the lotus; it is the promise of Nirvana, the promise of Nirvana, and a life that has broken the waters and brought forth the light of liberation.

The mani is not just a collection words. The vowels that are formed from the recitations of the mani are considered sacred. Buddhism has not dogmatized the mani, unlike institutionalized religious Faith systems. It is easy to recite. It is a completely democratic mantra. It is open to anyone who feels so inclined. It's even possible to recite it on the bus!

Vowels can also be vibrational, and when recited, they embody the compassion that indwells all that is, through vibrational sound. The mani's phonetic quality is harmonious and complete in itself. A world in pain needs nourishment from the sound, meaning, and quality of the vowels.

Siddhartha's 84,000 teachings can be found in six syllables within the mani. This makes it clear that the mani is perfectly formed. The mani is not just a collection or words, as I mentioned above. In fact, it is a microcosm for the spoken word as well as the sounds created by those words. It is not speech but the imitation of sounds. It doesn't matter if you understand the words. Meditation and a mindful meditation on the sounds is more important. The key to the ignition of the Great Vehicle Buddha mind is the mani. It ignites the love, compassion, and joy that naturally dwell in us.

This tension is beautifully expressed. We seek Nirvana, the extinguishment or complete extinction of our self. But we also want to infuse compassion. One fire, that of attachment, desire and suffering, is extinguished, so a new one is lit. We can feel compassion for the souls of others when we stop focusing on the self as the ultimate reality. Comppassion for oneself is the first step to compassion for others, and all of creation. Charity cannot be started at home. The lighting of the fire of compassion for yourself is the beginning of charity that can move anywhere but outward. Its tongues of fire rise higher and illuminate the darkness of a world where suffering can be extinguished by raising consciousness. Hope rises like sweet incense, an offering to the sufferer.

This mantra frees us from attachment to speech as a tangible expression and representation of our self and of being. We can let go of the idea that language is an expression of our worldviews or dogmas, and allow it to be the sound itself. This will enable us to feel sound as an expression and not as a form of being. It is our relationship to it in the way it has come from us. However, it is not an opinion or a thought. The mani, sound and pure compassion, is not ours but is part of our inheritance.

## The Six Syllables Of the Mani

The mantra, as we have learned, is the synthesis all of the Buddha's teachings. As unbelievable as it may sound, the six syllables contain the collective wisdom Siddhartha received under the Bodhi tree. Each syllable contains a small amount of wisdom. Understanding how each relate to a portion Buddha's lessons will enrich your mani experience and strengthen your connection to it.

Each syllable represents a paramita or teaching area that works to remove from your consciousness the spiritual vices that cause suffering. Six vices can be purified through the recitation each syllable.

The "om", the syllable that teaches generosity, guides you to a better understanding of its meaning and practice. Generosity does not mean giving away things or feeding, housing, and clothing people. All these are worthwhile pursuits. Generosity is a natural instinct to give back to others. Your spirituality and wisdom are within you. It is your love, peace, and joy. These are all qualities that you should be generous with, and increase them as you give them away. "Om" purifies your ego. It clings on to its dominant and greedy tendencies at your expense and those of others.

The second syllable "ma", which is the second vowel, refers to your ethical framework. It also describes how you treat other people. There is no ethical framework that does not include compassion. You should treat others with compassion and love. This is what "Ma" teaches and it helps you to get rid of jealousy, lust, and other negative emotions that can make others seem like pawns.

Your guide, "Ni", is the ability to develop patience with others (even those who are "difficult"), and your tolerance for differences and divergence. These qualities will be easier for the Buddhist practitioner who is trying to eliminate the self and its egotistical desire for primacy. We can cultivate patience and tolerance to temper our human passions that lead us to the insatiable wants that cause so much suffering.

The teacher of perseverance is the fourth syllable "pad". You recognize the inevitable wheel turning when you persevere. All is change, and you recognize that the uncontrollable reality of life is beyond your control. The ability to persevere in the knowledge of that everything is not as it seems is an attribute that is highly valued. It can be used to combat bigotry and ignorance, two of the most serious diseases in humanity.

"Me" refers to the perfection of concentration, and its role in your renunciation (and liberation) from all that causes suffering. Your little, distracted mind loves to wander around and kick over stones where suffering hides and attachment lurks. Focusing on your contemplative or meditative practice can bring you more peace, less attachment, and ultimately, reduce or eliminate all suffering. The key to freedom from the need for possessions and people at the expense or integrity of the delicately woven universe is renunciation.

"Hum" refers to the last syllable. It is the end of the syllable, and it represents the ultimate goal of Buddhist practice. Perfect wisdom is the ability to eliminate suffering and attachment, and attain Nirvana. This is the ultimate syllable that contains the Buddha's greatest teaching. The jewel of the lotus is a single sound, pronounced as part a chain of ancient teaching. It purifies our souls from hatred and aggression. It is impossible to hate or attack in perfect wisdom.

Reciting the Jewel in the Lot can help your mind to keep a consistent thought with all six syllables as well as the vowel sounds. Think about how compassion is being unleashed in all living creatures and how that compassion is reaching outward into all things. Relax in the tranquility that comes from peacefully observing your awareness. You are not attached or detached. You are abiding in your expansive temple of inner Buddha, sharing the teachings with all the universe.

# Chapter 4: Different Schools Of Buddhism

The Buddha's teachings were passed down through oral conventions for about 500 years, approximately 500 years after his death. They were first recorded in the Pali Canon, a group that was established in the second century BCE. As a way to disseminate his old knowledge, a variety of messages and interpretations were created.

Over hundreds of years, all major world religions have been organized into different groups, headings, and organizations. Buddhism is not an exception. There are three types of Buddhism: Hinayana Mahayana and Vajrayana.

Hinayana Buddhism

Buddha spent the last years of his life teaching in Northern India. He died at the age of 80.

The Four Noble Truths, Eightfold Path, Karma, and Nirvana are the core of Buddha's teachings. These Four Noble Truths only serve as an examination. They show that there is enduring life on this planet and that it can be overcome. Nirvana is the end of agony. It is a state of complete edification that is unmistakable and closes the cycle for resurrections. The Eightfold Path is an ethical guide that teaches people how to reach Nirvana.

Karma means that one is responsible for all outcomes. This implies that every person is responsible for his own actions. Early Buddhism doesn't believe that there is any divine being or holy person who can offer help. However, if one lives a decent, happy life, one can attain a higher state in the next life (resurrection or the idea of resurrections), until one reaches Nirvana, which is the ultimate joy. According to legend, the Buddha had 500 resurrections before he finally reached Nirvana.

Hinayana Buddhism was first spread in India, but it disappeared completely after being constrained by Hinduism and Islam trespassers. The early form of Buddhism can still be found in Sri Lanka, Cambodia, Myanmar and Thailand (Laos., Cambodia, Myanmar. Thailand. Vietnam).

Mahayana Buddhism

Hinayana, due to its very nature, was more of a theory than a religious system. Each individual was in control of his destiny. This idea is purely theoretical.

Buddha didn't need any devotion from anyone. Pictures of the Buddha are obscured in the midst of hundreds of years of Buddhism. Images were used.

A minister might have used the strong accentuation on contemplation to achieve edification (Nirvana), but it may not have been appropriate. This is what you might see for a common man. An agriculturist, who had to work hard in the fields from sunrise to daybreak. It was incompetent to be a mass-produced development because of its scholarly approach to Buddhism's early forms.

To make Nirvana's entrance easier, an entire group of small assistants was formed. These little assistants are known as Bodhisattvas.

Bodhisattva is a compassionate and understanding being who has at this time achieved Buddhahood (edification), but who refuses to go to Nirvana because there are still creatures on this planet who have not reached this state. They offer their compassion to others.

Bodhisattvas were presented with genuine photographs as tangible objects of love. Admirers could appeal to photos of the Buddha or an entire group of Bodhisattvas. As the old saying goes, a picture speaks louder than a thousand words.

Mahayana Buddhism was most popularly spread to the North, in Nepal, China and Mongolia. Around 100 A.C., Mahayana was improved. Mahayana is an acronym for "expansive vehicle". It was meant to show that it was suitable for certain people, while Hinayana ("little car") was more appropriate for a couple. Initially, the term Hinayana was somewhat disdainful.

Vajrayana Buddhism

Two attempts were needed to bring Buddhism to Tibet. The first was under King SongtsenGanpo (ruled between 630-649 AC), when he married a Nepalese princess and a Chinese princess. Both were active Buddhists who transmitted their faith to Tibet.

However, the Great Tibetan Empire ended with King Langdharma's death 200 years later. This marked the end of the primary period in Buddhism in Tibet. The highest ground was held by the first Bon religion, which is a shamanistic religion that is rich in devils and magicians.

Buddhism returned to Tibet in a momentary dissemination only after it took until the eleventh Century. It was an inseparable unit that included a sharp mixture of the old Bon religion. While the evil forces of the old world were declared defeated, they were also given another role as defenders for Buddhism. Beat them first, then coordinate with them for your particular purpose.

The result was Tibetan Buddhism, Vajrayana ("precious stones vehicle"), Tantric Buddhism or Lamaism. These terms all refer to a very similar type of Buddhism. It is a further development of Mahayana to this one-of-a kind, brilliant, and difficult to understand religious culture of Buddhas, gods holy people sages and masters.

This is it!

Clericalism is another important aspect of Tibetan Buddhism. The impact of religious communities in Tibet is greater than in any other country. An estimated 20% of Tibet's population lived in groups of friars or nuns before the Chinese communists took control.

Vajrajana includes not only parts of early Buddhism, but also shamanistic and administrative components. This is the mix that gave rise to Tibetan culture today, as it was created by the Tibetan evacuees, and their charismatic pioneer, the 14th Dalai Lama.

There are many types of sugar available these days, including dark colored sugars, white sugars, shake sugars, syrups, icing sugars, and syrups. However, all sugar tastes sweet. It comes in a variety of forms with the intention that it can be used in a variety of ways. Buddhism is one: There is Theravada Buddhism. Zen Buddhism. Pure Land Buddhism. Yogyakarta Buddhism. Vajrayana Buddhism. However, all Buddhism has the same path. Buddhism has evolved into many structures to be relevant to diverse societies.

This has been changed over the years to ensure that it is applicable in every era. Although the various forms of Buddhism might seem different, the core of each one is the Four Noble Truths (or the Eightfold Path). Each major religion, including Buddhism, has its schools and groups. The distinct Buddhist groups have never been at war and they still go to each others' sanctuaries and share their love. This kind of resilience and understanding is rare.

# Chapter 5: The Nature and Dztule of The Buddha'dz Teashing

Indztrustion by Buddha'dz is one of dzkillful adaption to the mood and concerns hidz hearerdz. He used the term ariua to describe the Sanskrit term that refers to the 'noble Aruan reorle in the dzendze for dzrirituallu noble and ennobled.

The Buddha dealt with questions with an analytic approach. Some he answered in direstlu; others he answered after analuzing them to slarifu their nature.

You can give them ur if you are certain that these ualitiedz will not lead to harm or suffering if they are pursued and blameworthy.

Accordingly, theu dzhould see that greed, hatred, and deludzion(lask of mental slaritu), which leaddz to behavior that harmdz otherdz, are to be avoided, and non-greed(generodzitu and renunsiation), non-hatred(loving kindnedzdz and somradzdzion)and non-deludzion(clarity of mind and wisdom)are to be engaged in.Bu imrlisation, teachings whish discourage the former and ensourage the latter are worth following.

The Buddha understood that hidz teashingdz were subject to a rrastisal, or rurrodze. He also said that a follower of the Buddha would not gradzr at Buddhist ideadz and practices but udze them for their intended rurrodze. This idz, a follower, would not gradzr at Buddhist ideasdz and practices but udze them to their intended rurrodze. However, many ordinary Buddhidztdz do have a dztrong attachment to Buddhism.

The Buddha was critical of blind faith but he didn't deny that there is a role for dzoundlu who badzed faith or 'trudztful confidzh' (dzaddha Skt sraddha); thudz to the exerle of thodze who have been well edztablidzhed in the Path.

# Chapter 6: The Teachings Of Buddhism

Some people do not consider Buddhism a religion because it does not allow for the worship of a god. The basic principles of Buddhism are simple and practical. Change is possible, everything in the world can be changed, and all actions have consequences. It is important to understand the Buddhist concepts. They can be applied to every individual's life regardless of race, gender, sexual orientation, nationality or gender. Buddhism is a system that teaches people practical methods to understand the world and their place within it. If put into practice, these teachings can change a person's whole life. Below are detailed explanations of the teachings of Buddhism.

The Way of Inquiry

Gautama Buddha cautioned against blind faith and encouraged people not to believe in the impossible. He knew the dangers of believing based on hearsay or tradition or because others believe it to be. He advised against blindly following ancient scriptures, even if one has faith in priests or elders. He encouraged people to be open-minded and to make their own decisions based on the world around them.

The Four Noble Truths

Buddha's teachings did not address the origin of the universe or philosophical speculations about God. They also didn't focus on heaven and eternal living in the afterlife. His teachings were centered on the reality of human suffering and the need for long-lasting relief from all types of distress and negative emotions. Buddha stated that the greatest human need was to find permanent relief from unhappiness and woe. These feelings can cause us to be in constant strife, and prevent us from living our best lives. He suggested that philosophical speculations are of secondary importance. They should be left behind until a person has trained their mind through meditation to a point where they can examine every situation more clearly and discover the truth.

The Four Noble Truths are the central teachings of Buddhism. These are the Four Noble Truths.

All living things are susceptible to sadness, disappointments, anxiety, discomfort, and other unpleasant emotions.

This is because of an insatiable desire that results from the illusion of a spirit.

Only by attaining enlightenment can this suffering be ended. This state allows a person to let go of the illusion that they are a soul. It will also allow them to end the suffering and cravings from their past.

You can achieve this peaceful and blissful enlightenment by regular practice of Buddhist techniques and following the Eightfold Path.

The Eightfold Path, or Middle Way

The Eightfold Path refers to the path that will lead all living creatures to freedom from suffering. It helps to avoid the extremes in self-mortification or sensual indulgence. Only when the body is in comfort, a state of calm and peace, can the mind be able to focus and meditate on the truths of the world. The Eightfold Path is about the cultivation of wisdom, virtue, meditation. It includes factors such as right understanding, right speech and right thought, right actions, right effort, right livelihood, mindfulness, and complete concentration.

Karma

Karma refers to our actions. Karma is a Buddhist concept that each of our actions produces inescapable consequences. Our speech, our thoughts, and the actions we take can all cause harm to us and others. These actions are known as "Bad Karma" or unwholesome. These actions are driven by unfounded desires, cravings, delusions, and ill will. Buddhism suggests that these actions can lead to painful outcomes and should be avoided in order for one to attain and sustain happiness, contentment, and mindfulness.

There are thoughts, actions, and spoken words that can help you and others. These positive outcomes are called "Good Karma" or wholesome. These positive emotions are the result of positive emotions such as generosity, wisdom, compassion. These deeds are said to bring good results and should be done as often as possible according to Buddhism.

Buddhism says that the outcome of one's Karma is what one experiences in life. When misfortune strikes, it is important to look at the faults in one's past behavior and not blame others. Reflecting on their own past actions can help one to see the root cause of the current situation. When one discovers the fault, they can take the necessary precautions to prevent it from happening again. The same goes for happiness. One can examine their past to see if there was Good Karma. If one can find the act that led to their happiness, they'll be able repeat it in the future to have more pleasant experiences. The old saying, "What goes around comes around" can sum up Karma.

Rebirth

Buddha claimed that he could recall many of his past lives with great clarity. Many Buddhist monks and nuns still claim to be able to recall their past lives. Deep meditation may help to achieve such a clear and powerful memory. Buddhists believe that if one can recall their past lives, then rebirth becomes more than a dream. It will be a certainty for them. This can help one see their present in a more meaningful way.

Buddha suggested that Karma should not be understood only in this lifetime, but across many lives. It may take several lifetimes for a person to bear the fruits their Karma. Karma and rebirth can be used to explain why certain children are born in different circumstances. For example, some babies are born to great wealth or good health, while others are born to poverty or illness. Good or Bad Karma can have an impact on the amount of pleasure or pain one feels or is experiencing. Buddha advised his followers to view any painful past experience as a lesson that they can use to improve their future actions (be it in this lifetime or the next), and not as punishment for their wrong deeds.

There is no Creator

Buddha suggested that all beings, including humans and gods, are subject to the law karma. Therefore, no one can be considered a supreme savior. Buddha was not able to save the world. Only the ability to point out truth led to wise people being able see it for themselves.

Buddha said that no God, living or non-living being, even religious leaders, can affect or interfere in another person's Karma. Buddhism encourages people to be fully responsible for their actions. Buddhists believe that to become successful or wealthy it is essential to be generous, diligent and hardworking. You must also be kind to others if you desire to reach the heavenly realm. You cannot ask for favors from God, and you can't commit unpunished corruption based on the law Karma.

The Illusion of a Soul

Buddhism says that there is no soul. What we refer to as a "living being" can only be described as a temporary assemblage of many activities and parts. These activities cease and the parts that are no longer relevant to each other, there is no living being.

A rebirth can occur even if there is no soul. Even though you may not have been with a soul in your previous lives, there is a causal connection between your current life and the past.

The root cause of suffering is often the illusion of a soul. This illusion manifests as "ego", which is the natural function to control our desire for happiness. This desire manifests itself as aversions or cravings that lead to an absence of inner harmony and peace. It also wants to control others and exploit the environment in order to gain possessions. Although its goal is to be happy, the ego always causes more suffering. This deep-rooted suffering can be ended only when the soul is understood to be a illusion. Your life is not more important than any other's. That is the hard truth.

Buddhism Today

Buddhism is now widely accepted in the world. Its acceptance extends far beyond its home country. People from all walks of the globe are choosing to practice Buddhism in a compassionate, peaceful and responsible way. Buddhism teaches that love, compassion, and tolerance are essential to a happy and peaceful life. These qualities are vital to being content. You can practice Buddhist meditation to formalize them.

Buddha said that the world outside is not enough to bring about lasting happiness.

He taught instead that the only way to achieve lasting happiness is to focus on one's inner world. Buddha said that a person's mind can be peaceful but not if they are happy inside. Only by understanding oneself and removing negative emotions, can one achieve a perfect state of mind.

# Chapter 7: Different Buddhist Traditions and How We Act on Our Practice

As we mentioned in the introduction Buddhism is a dynamic concept that changes with every culture that accepts it. There are many ways to practice Buddhism. However, they all share the same basic elements. This chapter will discuss some of the different ways Buddhist followers practice their faith in everyday life. It will also cover the traditions, customs and rituals that they use to stay mindful.

Buddhism is known for its tolerance, which means that these different practices can often work together to achieve similar goals.

It is not encouraged or required to rely on rituals in Buddhism. Rituals can help us define our spiritual motivations and allow us to continue on our spiritual journeys.

Karma's role as a practitioner

Many practices in Buddhism involve the idea of karma. This concept can be misunderstood today by newcomers to Buddhism. Karma isn't a metaphysical entity that punishes you for your wrongdoing. Karma is a practical concept.

Buddhist practitioners must avoid future suffering by abstaining from acts of harm to others, and instead promote future benefits through helping others. This is karma in action. It's quite simple.

Meditation and mindfulness

Apart from karma and the benefits of Buddhist rituals and practices, they are designed to help you focus your mind. Meditation, which we will discuss in a later chapter is an important aspect to Buddhism, is why it is so important. Meditation promotes mindfulness. This allows you to be more focused on the right actions and less on reacting to blind emotion.

You could, for example, take a variety of actions if you are at a drive-thru restaurant and the clerk at the counter makes a mistake. You could get mad at the person or throw the food at them.

This kind of behavior can lead to negative karma. You first upset the worker and cause them to suffer. A chain reaction of suffering follows as the worker's experience causes them to serve poor guests. You have created karma (a negative chain) by allowing yourself to be angry.

You don't feel better after engaging in negative behaviors. You may feel worse. Consider how you felt the last occasion you were truly angry or lost your temper. Your heart rate increases. Your blood pressure increases. The pressure can be felt in your head. It is possible to feel indigestion or a headache.

Your body will give you a physical response that shows you are suffering from your behavior.

You can break the cycle of negative karma by practicing mindfulness. Instead of blaming others, you can learn to be present and to pay attention to what is happening. Meditation is a way to practice mindfulness.

Prayer

Prayer and meditation are often compared. Some Buddhists enjoy praying alongside their meditation practice. While there is no right or wrong way to decide whether you include prayer in your Buddhist practice or not, certain Buddhist orders tend to consider prayer to be helpful.

Prayer is a common practice in the Tibetan order. Prayer wheels and prayer flags can be used to facilitate and magnify prayer. The physical effects of turning the wheel can increase one's awareness and ability to pray. The many words in a prayer flag flapping in wind can also provide mental magnificence of one's intent.

As the Buddha taught, it is important to look within yourself. If you find that prayer improves your mind control and helps you focus, then use it in your practice. You can train your mind by using rituals that challenge your ego-self.

## Chanting

Chanting can be used to meditate. Chanting is used often as a meditation tool. Chanting, like prayer and prayer tools helps one focus their mind.

Meditation can be made easier by having a sound and an act to focus on. Chanting can be used to boost positive intentions and motivate one, as well as clear the mind from negative views.

To focus their minds, some practitioners prefer to chant certain phrases like "Om". You can use any phrase for chanting. Chanting can be used in many situations in your daily life to prepare you for the rigors of the future.

## Vegetarianism

Vegetarianism is a popular practice among Buddhists. However, not all Buddhists practice it and it is not a requirement.

Shakyamuni wasn't strictly vegetarian, and he never forbade the consumption of meat. You'll see that there is one thing Buddhists have in common: a rejection for rigid rules. Buddhism's central tenet is that every individual must examine their own thoughts to determine the best course of action.

It is possible to abstain from meat occasionally, but it can be a spiritual practice. It can also be a tool to help you focus your thoughts and actions.

Many Buddhists consider the killing of animals to be a problem. Individuals deal with this issue in different ways. You can choose to only eat animals that were ethically raised and well treated. You might choose to give thanks to the animal that provided nourishment. You may also choose to limit your meat intake rather than being strict vegetarian.

Altars, incense and candles

Many Buddhist practitioners prefer to have a small meditation table in their homes. It is a place where one can remind themselves of their resolve to do right actions. It is a place where you can meditate and it reminds you to continue your practice. A visual reminder of our intentions is often helpful. You don't need an altar to meditate.

Your altar can be made of any material. You don't need to set up an altar in a specific way. You can set it up on a small shelf, a few blocks of cinder block, or even a small table.

You will find statues of Buddha, other figures, incense, candles, incense, bells, or beads on an altar for Buddhists. Each item serves the same purpose: to focus one's attention on the intention of meditation. If you use the same incense every time you meditate, it will prepare you for meditation by allowing you to smell the incense.

The Buddha figurines are not meant to be worshipped by Shakyamuni. The figurines are meant to remind us of the Buddha's teachings and example (dharma) and right action. It reminds you that the Buddha achieved enlightenment by practicing meditation, which is what you are about to do.

## Chapter 8: Approaching the Study

You may be a Christian, Muslim, Christian, Muslim or Atheist. However, you might find Buddhism confusing and mysterious. This guide will help you understand the basics of Buddhism and introduce you to the most effective spiritual path for you.

The first step to beginning a spiritual journey with Buddhism involves doing research. You've completed the first step in a sense because you are reading this guide. It's important to remember that Buddhism should be implemented in a way that works for you. You can follow the principles of Buddhism in the way you choose, just as different religions interpret the Bible in different ways. Buddha himself encouraged an individualistic approach, stating that you should accept the teachings according to your personal experience. You must approach Buddhism in a way you can understand.

Buddhism must be approached with patience and openness. Many people find that the complicated ideas of Buddhism take a while to unravel even after they start the journey. Although you can align yourself with Buddhist principles, you may need to take some time to understand the complex teachings. These feelings can be frustrating, but Buddhism encourages a philosophical outlook and deep questioning. This is a crucial experience in Buddhism. You might be asked question after question. You will eventually understand the mysterious nature of Buddhism, but for now, you can continue to question.

You should regularly pause to consider the meanings and implications of Buddhist teachings as you go through your spiritualistic journey. You must consider what each teaching means to you and how it fits into your life. You should take the time to reflect and meditate on these topics. We are often rushed to get information. Buddhism demands that we deconstruct such behaviors and adapt to a more contemplative way of thinking.

We now have a better understanding of Buddhism and can start to explore the various teachings. We'll be discussing some of the basic philosophical concepts associated with Buddhism in the next chapter.

# Chapter 9: Buddhist Teachings

The Four Noble Truths

These Four Noble Truths are the core of Buddha's teachings. While meditating beneath the Bodhi tree, the Buddha was made aware of the following Four Noble Truths: Dukkha (suffering), Nirodha [source of suffering], Magga ("path towards ending suffering") and Samudaya ("source of suffering"). These truths tell us that we can overcome the sufferings associated with human existence.

Dukkha (Suffering)

Our sufferings come in various forms. The three most obvious forms of suffering are the ones that Buddha saw when he left his luxury home: aging and illness. The Buddha believes that man's true sufferings go far beyond these three types of suffering. We are all susceptible to our desires and cravings. We crave more when we satisfy our cravings. Most of the pleasures we experience in life are temporary. They are usually temporary and, if they last, men find them boring and monotonous.

Many people don't experience grief or illness but still feel dissatisfied. This is true suffering, according to Buddha.

Samudaya (Source for Suffering).

There are definite causes to the daily discomforts and sufferings we experience, such as hunger, thirst and aches from illnesses and injuries, and grief at losing someone or something we value. The 2nd Noble Truth explains that all of our sufferings can be attributed to one cause: desire or tanha, which appears as the 3 Roots of Evil: greed (rooster), insanity (pig), and hatred (snake).

Nirodha (End of Suffering).

The Buddha teaches us that we can eliminate our attachments and desires. The Buddha teaches us in the 3rd Noble Truth that we can end our sufferings. He was also a living example of how it can be done within a man's lifetime.

Nirvana simply means "ending". The term "nirvana" or enlightenment means that you have ended all 3 fires of ignorance and greed. You won't suddenly disappear or move to another dimension. Nirvana can be described as a state of mind you can attain in order to experience deep spiritual happiness without any fears. A person who attains enlightenment is said to be filled with compassion for all living things.

It is believed that if you die after becoming enlightened, you will be free from the cycle of reincarnation. The Buddha does not give any details about what happens after an enlightened person dies. The Buddha actually discouraged his followers from asking many questions about nirvana. His followers should focus on reaching Nirvana, not what is next.

Magga (Pathway to End of Suffering).

The Buddha gave a remedy for man's sufferings in the last Noble Truth. The Eightfold Path, also known as the Middle Way, is the remedy. The Eightfold Path tells man to avoid extreme asceticism or extreme indulgence.

You are not supposed to follow the eight steps of the Middle Way in any particular order. Instead, allow the following steps and their complementing one another.

Samma ditthi (Right Understanding). Accept the teachings of Buddhism. The Buddha doesn't expect you to follow his teachings blindly. Instead, the Buddha expects you to learn and understand his teachings so that you can decide for yourself if they are true.

Samma sankappa (Right Intention). It is necessary to take the time to develop the right attitudes.

Samma vaca (Right Speech). Truthfulness is also a virtue. Avoid gossip, slanders, and other abusive speech.

Samma kammanta (Right Action). It is important to live in harmony and peace. It is not okay to steal, kill or indulge in sensual pleasures.

Samma ajiva (Right Livelihood). Do not live in a way that could cause harm or danger to other living creatures. Don't exploit others, kill animals or trade illegal substances or weapons.

Samma vayama (Right Effort). Positive thinking is essential. Negative and negative thoughts must be eliminated. Find out how to prevent these negative thoughts from returning in the future.

Samma sati (Right Mindfulness). It is important to be able to recognize your body, feelings and sensations, as well as your mental states.

Samma samadhi (Right Concentration). You must master your awareness by practicing mental concentration.

Karma

Karma is actually a belief shared by many religions of the East. Karma can be defined in different ways by different religions. Buddhism holds that the past actions you have taken can impact your future.

Karma is a concept that Buddhism taught earlier than the Tibetan Buddhism. Early writings suggested that not all the things we now experience are due to our past actions. According to the Tibetan teachings, everything that happens now is the result of our past actions. Even though there may be slight differences, all Buddhist teachings emphasize the importance of being aware of our motives and actions today to prevent future sufferings.

According to Buddhism, the consequences of karma can extend beyond our current lifetime. Negative actions you took in the past can be carried forward into the next life and cause negative consequences. Karma is the main factor in determining where and how you will be reincarnated. You may be reborn in the heavenly realm if you have good karma. Bad karma could result in you being reborn as an animal or in a hellish realm.

Therefore, a Buddhist tries to encourage good karma and avoid bad karma.

However, you must realize that Buddhism's real goal is to break the cycle of reincarnation. It is not about obtaining good karma.

Karma is a term that denotes "action", and it basically refers to a fundamental idea about karma. This means that your karma can be defined by your actions and the intentions behind them. Good karma is based on compassion, empathy, generosity, kindness and wisdom. Bad karma is based on ignorance, hatred and greed.

# Chapter 10: Nirvana - What is It and Why Is it Important in Buddhism

Nirvana is the ultimate goal of Buddhists. It represents the aspiration to achieve Enlightenment, and the freedom from the cycle of samsara. Nirvana in Buddhism is the state of the non-self (anatta) or of emptyness (sunyata). It is a state that is free from self-centeredness and desire. Many Buddhist scholars recognize two states of Nirvana, which are the "Nirvana with a Remainder" (sopadhishesa-nirvana) and the "Final Nirvana" (anupadhishesa-nirvana). It is believed that the First Buddha attained both of these states.

Nirvana, the ultimate goal of Buddhist practice, is one of the fundamental elements of Buddhist tradition. It is important, but it is not as simple as other elements of Buddhism. Nirvana, shrouded in mystery and subject to endless speculation, is a source of significant disagreement between various schools of Buddhist thought. Although the concept of

Nirvana has been widely accepted, specific details regarding its nature are left up to each individual. Nirvana, an aspect of Buddhism, serves to bring Buddhism together with other non-Buddhist traditions. It also allows for differences of opinion within the Buddhist community. This makes Nirvana one of the few true mysteries in the Buddhist tradition.

One of the reasons Buddhism is so mysterious is that Buddha clearly defined the basic principles of Buddhism in his teachings. The Four Noble Truths provide a clear explanation of the nature of suffering and life in such a simple way that there is no room for confusion. It is simple to understand that cravings lead to suffering and that the Eightfold Path can help one eliminate their cravings and eliminate all suffering. The problem is that Buddha didn't go into as much detail in describing Nirvana than he did in describing other things. Even worse, Buddha didn't encourage contemplation of Nirvana or speculation about it. The Buddha's teachings place all attention on the present and the actions one takes at that moment.

This focus was designed to ensure that people would reach Nirvana by taking care of the present. It is possible to be dangerous thinking about Nirvana. One thing is that the more time someone spends contemplating Nirvana, the less they will spend focusing their attention on the present moment. This is against the Buddhist traditions, so it is understandable that Buddha wouldn't encourage speculation like this. If a person is motivated to attain Nirvana by perfecting their actions, then there will be a self-serving element. If a person is focused on the Eightfold Path for the sake of the Path, then their actions will be selfless. If the goal is to attain Nirvana then there is a chance for personal gain. The idea of seeking Nirvana is dangerous because it leads to personal gain and craving. Buddha spoke enough about Nirvana in Buddhism to make it a part of Buddhist tradition.

However, it should not be so overwhelming that it becomes a hindrance for other Buddhist practices.

## The Basics of Nirvana

Everyone can agree on the meaning of Nirvana. Nirvana literally translates to "cooling off" or "blowing out". Although there is much speculation and debate about the exact reason Buddha used this word to describe a specific state of being, it is widely accepted that it refers the elimination of suffering. This life is often referred to as the fires and suffering of attachment and craving (dukkha), which cause suffering. The same feeling can also be observed in modern terms, outside of Buddhist traditions. These terms, such as "heat of passion" or "fiery ambition", convey the same imagery that Buddha spoke so many centuries ago. The Eightfold Path is the way to get rid of these passions and ambitions. It stands to reason that a successful journey along the Path will result in those fires being put out. In the context of eliminating those things that cause suffering, terms such as 'cooling down' and 'blowing out" make perfect sense.

A third aspect of Nirvana that almost everyone agrees on is the idea that it is a destination you can move towards. This is especially true in the Eightfold Path. It is not a good idea to follow a path that doesn't take you somewhere. Anyone who is committed to the Eightfold Path must envision a life that is free from the suffering and pain associated with it. As someone wouldn't hesitate to drive down a road they don't know the end of, so would anyone who wants to follow the Eightfold Path. It is generally agreed that there are two main paths to Nirvana. The Eightfold Path is the first. This is the Eightfold Path. A person gradually moves towards Nirvana by following the Eightfold Path's instructions. Enlightenment is the second step to Nirvana. It can take years to attain this path, as with the Eightfold Path. However, it can be achieved in a matter of minutes. No matter how fast or slow a person attains enlightenment, one thing is certain: it will lead them to Nirvana. Even if for just a moment. Here is where the agreement about Nirvana ends.

Nirvana with the Remainder

The Nirvana without a Remainder, as it is known in ancient Buddhist texts, refers to the achievement of nirvana – freedom from samsara – within a single life. This occurs when all three fires (Delusion, Confusion, Greed, Sensual Attachment and Aversion or Will) are extinguished. There is still some of the five Clinging Aggregates. However, it is not "burning" and is only ashes. Richard Gombrich, a Buddhist scholar defined the Five Clinging Aggregates as the firewood that fuels the Three Fires. To stop the firewood from fueling the Three Fires the aspirant must make an effort to give up. This will allow one to reach Nirvana, the ultimate state of being free from all suffering, desires, and self-deprecating behavior. Only then can you experience complete happiness. The Enlightened Ones who attain Nirvana with the Remainder experience blissful happiness and a transformed mind that is completely free from all negative mental states. It is difficult for humans to understand this concept because if you try too hard, you lose your ability to let go. This letting go allows you to see what you need to get to Nirvana. This concept is still far from being understood.

The result of enlightenment is almost always Nirvana with the Remainder. This happens almost without warning or expectation, much like enlightenment. It is not possible to assume that six years of meditation was enough time for Buddha to attain enlightenment. While enlightenment may be possible in a short time for a few lucky people, it can take a lifetime or longer for most people. It doesn't matter how long it takes for enlightenment to happen, it's a sudden and immediate experience. Enlightenment can be described as a quick and thorough process, similar to turning on a light switch. Enlightenment is not a feeling of learning new knowledge but of losing your ignorance. A person who experiences enlightenment feels like they have lost their false sense of themselves and are now able to see clearly. The ultimate sense of self can affect how one relates to others and the entire universe. This all-encompassing state is similar to being in another world but still being within the physical world. This is Nirvana, a state that brings oneness with all living creatures to a higher level.

Nirvana with the Remainder has one advantage: the person who attains this state can share their experience with others. This phenomenon is probably best illustrated by the Buddha. Buddha spent the rest of his life sharing his newly acquired knowledge with everyone who would listen after he had achieved enlightenment. This is very similar to the Jesus tradition. Many traditions tell of a person who undergoes a real transformation, then spends the rest of their life helping others. It would be unrealistic to expect anyone to achieve Nirvana with a remaining person to do so. However, it is possible to have a huge impact on others in your life, healing all kinds of wounds and eventually guiding them on the path to self-discovery, and ultimately, enlightenment. This is the same as a person being able to reach Nirvana without dying and then helping others.

Nirvana without Remainder

You will probably have an idea of how to reach Nirvana without Remainder after learning about Nirvana and the Remainder. This is the last Nirvana, where the Enlightened One "flashes out" at the end his life. There is no more fuel. This is also the Buddhist equivalent to Heaven. As Heaven is a Christian concept that a righteous soul achieves a higher state after being separated from their body by the process death, so Nirvana with no Remainder is the idea that the individual's consciousness is completely free from all the sufferings in the physical realm due to death. This aspect of Nirvana is what unites Buddhism and other non-Buddhist traditions. This idea of an afterlife gives Buddhism a religious appearance. It is similar to Christianity, Islam, Judaism, and many other traditions that believe in a spiritual afterlife. This is the most significant difference between the different Buddhist traditions.

The idea of Nirvana being a kind of afterlife is problematic because it does not consider the existence of a soul. Many Buddhist traditions don't believe in a soul like other traditions. A person is not believed to have a permanent spiritual identity. Instead, they are thought to be made up of pure energy. The experiences that a person has in a given life are what create their identity. According to this tradition, Nirvana refers more to a person becoming 'free' from the ego and self-centeredness that prevented them from being one in the divine source. A drop of water in an ocean ceases being the ocean. The same applies to individuals who cease to be part of the divine whole. Nirvana refers to the feeling of an individual's energy merging with the divine and becoming part of the whole again. It is similar to the drop of water being returned into the ocean, where it will never again be found. This tradition teaches that true suffering is caused by a feeling of separation from all other living creatures. Attachment, craving and other causes of suffering are just extensions of the true cause of suffering which is a feeling of separation from all living things. A person can be freed from the experience of physical separation from God. This will allow them to free themselves from the fires and cravings of ego, desire, and the rest.

Reincarnation is another issue with Nirvana without Remainder. Many traditions believe this is the ultimate destination. However, some traditions of Buddhism believe that karma may be able to supersede Nirvana with Remainder. This means that even if an individual attains Nirvana, they still need to compensate for any bad karma. Bad karma could be from the current life or from past lives that still needs to be atoned. This is where things get a little tricky. A person who doesn't possess a soul as such can't carry on karma from previous lives. If Nirvana is the ultimate release of a person from their individual status, then how can they keep individual karma? This may be why Buddha chose to concentrate on other aspects of his life than Nirvana. Who can really know all the answers?

Nirvana in Nutshell

Although many of these details may seem contradictory or confusing, it is the accepted belief that someone who attains Nirvana does not automatically become free from all karmic obligations. Some believe that someone with unresolved karma will not reach full Nirvana. They will not experience the transcendence and pure joy, but will still be just below full integration with God. They will only be able to reunite with the divine source of their life again after they have fully paid off their karmic debts.

This demonstrates the true nature and purpose of Nirvana. Nirvana, unlike the Heaven of Christianity and other afterlife destinations, is not considered a physical location. Nirvana can be described as a state or state of being. It can be attained before or after death. Nirvana with the Remainder is a case where a person can drift into and out of Nirvana in much the same way as a person could go into or out of a particular room in their home. This is especially true for those who attain Nirvana by enlightenment. Although the Buddha experienced what could be called "enlightenment without a capital E", there are smaller doses of enlightenment that could be described as "enlightenment without a little e". It is possible that the Nirvana experienced by those who have achieved a lower level of enlightenment would be temporary. Because they are still striving for perfection in other areas of their lives, they wouldn't be able to attain full Nirvana. Because Nirvana refers to a state of being and is temporary, any less would be temporary than permanent.

Understanding Nirvana can help to clarify the many elements that can make Nirvana so confusing. This is why Nirvana can be experienced after death. As someone who achieves Nirvana while they are still alive might still have lessons to be learned, so too can someone who experiences Nirvana after death. This allows you to reconcile Nirvana with reincarnation in a reasonable amount of any mindset. The best way to see it is to picture the Path as a hilly path. A person can climb a hill to see Nirvana from the distance and experience temporary Nirvana. As they descend the hill, Nirvana can be a source of immense excitement and inspiration. When Nirvana has been reached, there is no other path, and the person has achieved the ultimate goal.

However, even then, one can choose to stay in the cycle of Samsara and return in physical form to share their love and knowledge with others who are suffering in the physical realm. This would explain why people like the Dalai Lama exist. He should not have any outstanding karmic debts or lessons to learn that would prevent him from reaching total Nirvana. People who are more than humans are a common theme in traditions all over the globe. This could be evidence that such enlightened people choose to stay on this plane of existence to aid humanity's return to unity with God. These people are not giving up on Nirvana as much as they might think. They may be experiencing Nirvana in full, even though they are still physically present. This is the most significant difference between Nirvana and any other tradition of a paradise. Although this life is meant to lead to Nirvana it can still be lived. This is one of many wonderful ways Buddhism is more than a promise or belief system. It is possible to attain Nirvana in this lifetime, and it can also be experienced continuously in this lifetime, so there is no separation between the non-physical and physical realities. The question of Nirvana remains. Is Nirvana not just about the transformation of an individual? If enough people attain full Nirvana can they effect a complete transformation of human life? Is it possible for the entire world to experience the same transformation that the person living there? The answer is not available for everyone.

# Chapter 11: Meditation as an Integral Part of Buddhism

Meditation is an integral part Buddhism. Some would even say it is the foundation of Buddhism. Siddhartha discovered meditation through which he was able to relax, let go of his own thoughts and accept the suffering without getting too angry. To make Buddhism an integral part of your daily life, every Buddhist should follow this example.

After you have gotten up, brushed your teeth, and eaten a nutritious meal, you can start your first meditation. You will need to find a quiet spot in your home. It doesn't need to be fancy or anything, but it should allow you to focus. After you've found the right spot, take a cushion or a pillow and relax. This is the essence of meditation.

You can now take the lotus position, and focus your attention on your body. Meditation is a form of relaxation. It requires intense concentration. To achieve this, we will be focusing on each part of our bodies until we feel one with all cells of our being.

Concentrate first on your hands. Next, channel that relaxation down your arms and down your sides to your thighs. Then, focus on how it feels when you sit down on the cushion (or whatever surface you are using) until this sensation extends to the floor.

This will allow you to achieve a deep level of concentration and a precise fixation on time and space. After you are able to tune in to your spatial positioning, pay attention to your breathing. Next, exhale slowly and focus on the air leaving your lungs. Take another inhale and exhale, focusing on your breathing as it leaves your lungs. As you go, you will build a rhythm. This will increase our relaxation response and help us to start our day relaxed.

After your morning meditation has been completed, you can now focus on maintaining the same state of mindfulness throughout your day. Try to maintain a steady focus on all your daily activities, from the moment you get up to the moment. Focus on your body's needs so that you can stand up even if you are sitting down.

As you take your first steps, pay attention to the movement of your feet as you walk. As you approach the door, do not just walk through it, but acknowledge that you will be going through the door before actually doing so. This may seem strange to someone just starting Buddhism. However, it is this high-tuned state of mindfulness that can help you take meditation seriously and make it an integral part your life.

# Chapter 12: How did Buddhism originate?

Buddhism was established in the sixth century B.C. Prince Siddhartha, a Northeastern Indian prince, founded Buddhism. According to Buddhism's history, Prince Siddhartha became determined to find an answer to the suffering of the world after he saw it.

Although there are many versions of the story about Prince Siddhartha becoming the Buddha, historians agree that Buddhism had a founder. It didn't happen by accident. The actual documentation of Prince Siddhartha's life was not available until three centuries after his death. The details in the following story are the most common and accepted story about how, where, and when Buddhism began.

The Buddha's Beginning

According to legend, Prince Siddhartha's birth was predicated by a holy man. He predicted that Prince Siddhartha would become one of the two things. Young Prince Siddhartha would become either a great spiritual leader, or a great military conqueror. His mother, King Suddhodana (leader of the Shakya clan), had died before he was born. Therefore, Prince Siddhartha was to be trained according to his wishes. Prince Siddhartha was protected from all religions and suffering, and was taught how to conquer war by military leaders.

Prince Siddhartha, at the age of 29, was overcome by curiosity and asked a charioteer for rides to the countryside. He saw an old man, a sick man, and then a corpse on his trips. Prince Siddhartha was struck by the harsh realities of life and became heartbroken. On his fourth outing, Prince Siddhartha spotted a wandering ascetic. The charioteer explained to Prince Siddhartha that an ascetic is someone who has renounced all worldly offerings and seeks freedom from fear and suffering.

Prince Siddhartha retreated to his life of luxury, but he found it difficult to enjoy anything. Prince Siddhartha, the son of his wife, was not able to find joy even after he gave birth to him. Prince Siddhartha woke up one night and thought about the death, old age and disease that would soon overtake him and make his body a dusty mess. He knew he couldn't live the life of a prince, or a great military mind. He shaved off his hair that night and changed into a ragga robe to leave his family and home to pursue his quest for enlightenment.

The Search of the Buddha

Prince Siddhartha began his journey by looking for renowned teachers. These teachers taught him about various religious philosophies and how to meditate. Prince Siddhartha didn't find the answers to his questions after learning all that the teachers had taught him. He remained unsure and had many questions. He left with five of his disciples to continue their quest for enlightenment.

Prince Siddhartha, his companions, sought relief from their suffering by disciplining their physical selves. They suffered extreme pain, ate roots and berries until they died. Prince Siddhartha discovered that he was still not satisfied. He realized one day that he had abandoned pleasure to grab onto pain. In essence, he had moved from one extreme to another. Prince Siddhartha believed there had to be a middle way between these extremes.

After some reflection, Prince Siddhartha realized the only way to liberation was through discipline of the mind. He realized that he should not starve, but nourish his body and increase his strength. His companions saw Prince Siddhartha accept a bowl of rice milk offered by a young woman. They assumed he was abandoning their quest and left him to continue their journey.

The Buddha's Enlightenment

After wandering about for a while, Prince Siddhartha decided that he would sit under a sacred tree fig. This became the Bodhi Tree, and he settled down to meditation. Bodhi is a Greek word meaning 'awaken'. Some versions of the story say that Prince Siddhartha sat down for seven days. Other versions don't give a time frame.

Legend has it that the Work of Prince Siddhartha was done while he meditated. It is often referred to as a battle with Mara, the demon whose name means "destruction." Mara is the symbol of all passions that can snare or deceive us. Mara sent large armies full of monsters to attack Prince Siddhartha. He was not affected by the attacks. Mara sent his most beautiful child to try to seduce Prince Siddhartha. She was also unsuccessful. Mara finally told Prince Siddhartha the seat of enlightenment was his. The demon claimed that his spiritual achievements were more than Prince Siddhartha. Mara's monsters shouted "I am his witness!" Mara challenged Prince Siddhartha to "Who will speak for me?" Prince Siddhartha reached down and touched the earth with his right hand. The earth responded by roaring, "I bear your witness!" Mara disappeared. As the sun rose in heaven, Prince Siddhartha saw the light of the sun and realized that he was now Buddha.

Sharing the Word of Enlightenment

The Buddha hesitated at first to share what he had learned from his Enlightenment. It was difficult to communicate his realizations in words. Delusions must be thrown away in order to experience the Great Reality. It would take discipline and mental clarity. He was certain that anyone listening to his words would be misunderstood if they didn't have the experience to attain Enlightenment.

He was moved by his compassion to share what he knew. The Buddha found the five companions that had abandoned him prior to his enlightenment and preached his first sermon to them. Instead of giving doctrines about enlightenment, the Buddha showed a path of daily practice that would enable people to attain enlightenment.

Happiness is not about forcing people to believe what they believe. It's about educating them. Buddha believed it was important that people question everything to discover their answers.

He dedicated his entire life to teaching, and quickly attracted hundreds upon hundreds of followers. He eventually came to terms with his father, who had left his home and abandoned his family. His wife was soon a nun and a disciple. His son, aged seven years old, became a novice monk. He lived with his father all his life. The Buddha traveled the world and taught until his death in eighty. The word of Buddhism has spread throughout the globe and most people are familiar with the Buddhist way to live.

## Chapter 13: The Rules Of Karma

Karma, which is translated to mean "action", is the fundamental order of the universe. Karma is about your intentions and the consequences of your actions. The universe will return whatever you put into it. We must pay attention to how our actions impact the world around us.

We create suffering by our actions of hate, selfishness, and greed. We can lay the foundation for a life filled with fulfillment if we act with kindness, mindfulness, and wisdom.

3 poisons:

These three poisons, or Three Unwholesome Roots, are the source of all suffering, negativity and bad karma. They are Moha and Dvesha and Lobha which translate to ignorance, hate and greed.

Moha - Ignorance

"Where ignorance is our master there is no chance of real peace."

-His Holiness, the Dalai Lama

According to the ancient Chinese belief, ignorance is the root of all evil. It is ignorance to the Four Noble Truths, which can lead to someone's death. Neglecting the impermanence of life can lead to some dangerous actions. Ignorance is the poison that causes hate.

Hate - Dvesha

"Holding onto anger is like grasping at a hot coal with an intent to throw it at someone else; you're the one who gets burnt." -Buddha

Because we are unable to comprehend, hatred arises out of ignorance. We find it difficult to see ourselves and the universe together and instead fall for the illusion of a separate self. We want the things we don't have, and we resent those who prevent us from getting them. Hate is the poison that leads to separation.

Greed - Lobha

"... A man who lives a simple life can't be destroyed. He can conquer greed and no one can stop him from being free.

-Buddha

Even the most morally upright people can be corrupted by greed. It can take control of our thoughts and actions, as if it were a chain that holds us down. Greed, desire and need drive us into a cycle of suffering in which we continue to search for support but fail to find it. This is what causes us to harm others in order to make ourselves better. It's focusing on your survival, and not the survival of others. Greed is the poison that makes our world run on misery.

So now you know the basics... what's next?

You have now learned the basics of Buddhism. But that's only half of your journey. To gain insight about yourself and the universe, you need to look within. It is now time to put in the effort to take the right actions to truly be enlightened.

Although it has been a long time since Buddha was alive in this world, many things have changed. His teachings still hold true today. It is difficult to concentrate when there are so many distractions, such as smartphones and technology. It's possible to still follow the Eightfold Path, despite this. Now, we will discuss everyday stress and how to manage them.

Addiction

Our constant yearning for more can lead to addiction and make it difficult for us to find the path of awakening. We want to fill the void inside so we resort to drugs, alcohol and food.

Attachment and. The illusion of self

"...how does self-attachment and other such phenomena arise with such force? The mind is unable to let go of 'I' and this leads to the creation of self-attachment. The lack of knowledge about the nature of things leads to a false notion of 'I'. This obscures the fact that all objects have no inherent existence and leads to one's strong conception of 'I.' The afflicting ignorance that phenomena exist inherently is what is responsible for all afflictions ..."

-Dalai Lama

According to the dictionary, addiction can be loosely described as a dependence on a substance or stimulation. According to Buddhism, addiction can be described as an attachment to intoxicants to alleviate suffering. If we take intoxicants and develop a preference for them, we are pulling away from enlightenment. We also become more attached to the world. Attachment can cause us to feel empty because all things are temporary. This sense of unfulfillment, or emptiness, is what keeps us in a depressive cycle of giving in to stimulants and falling further from true enlightenment.

Suffering

This addiction is when your attachment causes suffering. The Eightfold Path and the precept to abstain from intoxicants are violated by the misuse of these intoxicants. This attachment can make us a slave to our own thoughts and actions, and we lose all control over ourselves. We are enslaved by intoxicants and our own thoughts.

Addiction can give us the illusion of no choice. But that is far from reality. It is hard to make a change and it takes constant effort. But, change is the only way out.

Acceptance

Accepting that your suffering and thirst are the root causes of your suffering is the first step. Recognize that you have a problem keeping you from reaching your full potential. It is crucial that you recognize the consequences of your actions on your spiritual and physical health. You must also accept the fact that you may need treatment or meditation to break free from your addiction. You will regain control of your life once you have put forth the right effort and taken the right actions.

## Questions about Marriage

Even if you are a Buddhist, problems in a marriage are a part of everyday life. Attachment is the root cause of all suffering. Therefore, a strong attachment to another person will cause problems. These problems may be caused by trust issues, misunderstandings or the in-laws.

Although marriage may make our lives more difficult, it is not forbidden. Buddha often spoke about marriage in his teachings, including what we should expect from our partners as well as how to please our inlaws.

## Self understanding and selflessness

Most marital problems stem from our inability or unwillingness to listen to our partners. It is important to be aware of how our actions affect our partners. It is important to observe the actions of our partners and their effects on us. A great way to deal with problems in a relationship is to have self-understanding.

We are made to be selfish as mortals. However, this selfishness only leads to emptiness, suffering, and insecurity. Selfishness in marriage reinforces the illusion that we are separate from our spouses. We should instead see ourselves as one with the entire universe, including our spouses.

What to Expect From Marriage

False expectations or misunderstandings can cause marital problems. It's crucial to understand what your partner expects from you and what you should expect from them.

Buddhist teachings explain what a wife can expect from her husband and what she should expect from him. The husband should expect his wife to love him, be faithful, provide meals and childcare, and have a sweet and soothing personality. The husband should expect his wife to be loyal, honest, trustworthy, moral support, and friend.

It is best to keep in mind that teaching should be a suggestion, not an obligation. It is important to have these qualities in order to maintain a balanced marriage.

## Money, Money and More Money

Money is often viewed as the root of all evil. However, it is not. Money is only a temporary thing that can be made evil by our greed and obsessiveness. Although the Buddhist teachings on attachment and materialism would lead you to believe that money is not a topic we discuss, there are many teachings!

## Budgeting

Although it would be wonderful to have all our possessions gone and live a free life, this is not possible in the real world. Even in the most prosperous times, this causes problems to continue to grow.

To avoid stress, you must budget according to the Buddhist method. This means being aware of what you have and what you don't. Take stock of the things you don't need and get rid of them. Spend less on unnecessary things to simplify your life. You don't need everything.

## Financial stress

Money is a source of stress, and we cannot avoid it. We can learn to manage anxiety. We must be aware of all the Noble Truths and remember the First Truth. All suffering is temporary, and all financial problems are temporary. No matter how much money you make, money will not be enough to alleviate that anxiety.

## Giving with money

Spending excess money in excess is not the best way to spend it. Donate to a worthy cause and practice generosity. Don't let money be a negative influence on your life. Instead, make it a positive force in your life.

## Emotions

We can become a slave to our emotions through things like anger, envy, greed, desire, or even jealousy. It doesn't mean we should suppress our worldly emotions. Rather, we need to accept and understand our emotions. It is important to recognize the root cause of negative emotions and learn how to let them go.

Mental and emotional Illness

Mental illness is not curable by willpower alone. Sometimes meditation alone is not sufficient to treat mental illness. Many programs offer similar treatment methods to the Eightfold Path, and some even cater specifically towards Buddhists. You can gain freedom from your suffering by seeking treatment or guidance.

Many people believe Buddhism will discourage followers from using antidepressants or anti-anxiety medications. However, this is a common misconception. Buddhism is all about balance, and medications can help to balance an unbalanced head.

Depression

Depression can result from many things in our lives. It can even be unbearable if we have the Four Noble Truths. Depression can make us feel worthless, demotivated, and disconnected from the world. You can make steps to rid yourself of any bad karma and get out of depression. You can also learn the Four Noble Truths and keep them in your mind often.

These mantras can be used to help you deal with these feelings while you meditate.

This is a moment to be kind to me.

I am one with all things. I am one with all things.

This is a time of suffering. This too will pass.

Anxiety

Anxiety can be caused by the feeling of emptiness and attachment to things that make us feel a part of something. Anxiety is caused by fear of losing them. If you don't fully grasp that all things are temporary, anxiety is inevitable. It is important to learn to see the present and not the future.

These mantras can be used to help you deal with these feelings while you meditate.

Breathe in and out.

Do not be afraid There is no danger.

I am safe. I am secure. I don't have to worry.

Anger

Even the most passive person can become aggressive monsters by anger. Anger can cause us to lose sight of the important things and become blinded by rage. Anger can turn to anger, but ignorance can lead to hatred or greed. Accepting your anger is important and allowing it to go in accordance with the Eightfold Path.

These mantras can be used to help you deal with these feelings while you meditate.

I am calm. I feel at peace.
I am one in the universe.

## Chapter 14: Buddhist Temples

What is a Buddhist Temple?

A Buddhist temple is a place where Buddhist believers can practice meditation and worship together. Buddhist temples are distinguished by their unique history, the presence of monks and impressive architecture, as well as their spiritual atmosphere. Every Buddhist temple has a statue or image of Buddha. There are also common elements in every temple that represent the five elements: Fire, Wisdom (Air, Water), Wisdom (Water), and Earth. The temple's pinnacle symbolizes wisdom, and the square base represents earth. When they visit temples, Buddhists observe the correct ethics. These are the proper etiquettes, such as how to take photos, dress appropriately, and interact with monks. Buddhists worship shrines at their homes or at stupas. Shrines are stone structures that house their scriptures and relics.

What is a Pagoda and how does it work?

A pagoda is a Buddhist temple. Buddhists gather in pagodas on full moon days and during festivals to chant hymns.

Pagodas are typically made of wood and have many tiers. There are many shapes available. They include statues of Buddha and candles in the pagoda along with incense burners.

It was built near a guesthouse. These pagodas were used as places of worship and rest by Buddhist monks who traveled far and wide in ancient times.

Are you a Buddhist worshipper?

There are two kinds of worship. Worshipping a God is a time when we give thanks and honor Him. We offer offerings to God and ask for His favors. We believe the God will answer our prayers and hear our praises. Buddhists, on the other hand, do not practice such worship. Second, people worship by showing respect for someone or something they admire. It's like when a teacher enters the classroom. We stand up. A person shakes hands with a dignitary when he or she meets him. When the national anthem is played, we salute. These gestures are expressions of reverence and respect and show our admiration for particular things or peoples.

The Buddha statue, with its hands resting in its laps, reminds us to cultivate love and peace within ourselves. The lamp reminds of the light of knowledge and reminds us that flowers will soon fade and die, reminding us of impermanence. Bowing is a way for someone to express his inner feelings. It's a sign of gratitude to Buddha for the teachings he has given us. This is the essence of Buddha's worship.

Three of the Most Famous Buddhist Temples on the Planet

Borobudur

It's located on Java, an Indonesian island. It is located 25 miles northwest of Yogyakarta and is the most well-known Buddhist temple in the entire world. It was built by the kingdom Sailendra in the 8th and the 9th centuries. It was built from 2 million blocks of stone. Borobudur was abandoned in the 14th Century for unknown reasons. Under layers of volcanic ash, the jungle hid Borobudur for centuries.

Bagan

Bagan is the second-most famous Buddhist temple. It is also known as Pagan. It lies on the banks the Ayerwaddy River. This river is home to the largest number of Buddhist temples, ruins, and pagodas anywhere in the world. The capital of many ancient Burmese kings built 4,400 temples between 1000 and 1200. After refusing to pay Kublai Khan tribute, the kingdom was lost to Mongols. Bagan was then quickly lost as a political centre. It continued to thrive as a center for Buddhist scholarship.

Shwedagon Pagoda:

Shwedagon Pagoda (also known as Golden Pagoda), is located in Yangon. It is the most revered Buddhist temple and is also the holiest Buddhist shrine of Burma. Its origins Shwedagon have been lost in antiquity. It is believed that the Pagoda was built first by the Mon in the Bagan period. It was built sometime between the 6th to 10th centuries AD. The temple is filled with colorful and glittering stupas but the main 326-foot high main stupa is the centre of attention. The entire stupa is covered in gold.

The Buddhist Beliefs

Buddhists believe many things. Some beliefs may be about Gods, Ancestors and the afterlife. The most important beliefs of Buddhists concern suffering and troubles, and how to overcome them. This is because Buddha wanted to be a Buddha when he first visited the city, where he saw people who had suffered from sickness, birth, and death.

We all know Gautama Buddha was the "Enlightened one." When he was enlightened, he taught how to end suffering. It all starts with understanding the true nature and purpose of the universe.

Buddha saw knowledge as only necessary if it is practical. Buddha disapproved of speculations about God, the nature and afterlife. His followers were encouraged to concentrate instead on the Four Noble Truths, which can help them get rid of all troubles and problems in life.

Buddhas and deities

Celestial buddhas and bodhisattvas are all around the world. They are a source of inspiration and help the Buddhist practitioner. Kuan Yin is the Medicine Buddha, Kuan Yin the Medicine Buddha, and the Laughing Buddha. This segment also contains charming characters and others.

The Nature of an Individual

Hinduism refers to the soul (or atman) as a spiritual entity or being that is eternally existing and moves between bodies at renewal. This theory was denied by Buddha.

## The Purpose of Your Life

Buddhism teaches that the goal of life should be to eliminate misery. According to Buddha, humans are miserable because they keep trying to find permanent satisfaction in things that don't work.

## Resurrection & Immortality

Buddha said, "Life is a journey. Death is a return to the earth." The universe is like an inn. The passage of time is like dust. This delusional world is like a star rising, a bubble within a rivulet and Thunderbolt in the summer cloud. It's an illusion and a dream.

## It's never too late to start

Many Buddhist Schools stress the fact that enlightenment can be achieved in a matter of minutes. Other schools emphasize the fact that enlightenment can be a slow process and may take many lifetimes. Both agree that it's never too late for people to start learning and practicing the right way of life. The more educated a person is, they will suffer less. It's never too late.

This famous quote states that:

Even if you are going to die tomorrow

Be positive and keep your head clear.

Keep your life happy, day after day.

All of you will eventually attain the highest happiness of Enlightenment

(Lama Yeshe)

Strive for Balance

According to the book "Middle Way", if you tighten the string too tightly, it will snap. It will also not play if it is left too wet.

Buddha taught that one should not be too strict with others. Moderation is key to success.

It is important to show compassion

Compassion is the natural existence and expression of wisdom and understanding. We become wiser when we have compassion.

Buddha said, "If we light a lamp to help someone, we also light our way."

It's good to be kind

Buddhists believe that what we do to other people will eventually affect us.

Buddhism encourages good deeds but does not require that you follow rigid rules. It is up to each individual to decide the best course of action to ensure their happiness for the long-term. Buddhists offer five precepts that can help you take actions that lead to positive outcomes. These precepts are:

You can't lie

Steal or defraud

Injure or kill others

Sexual relationships can cause pain

Do not confuse your mind with intoxicants

Our bodies are precious

The life of a human being is regarded as very precious. To live a long and happy life, it is a rare opportunity. It is vital that we keep our health in good shape.

It is our responsibility to keep the body healthy. We will not be able keep our minds clear and active if we don't.

It's up to us.

Buddhism says it is not upto others to make us learn. We are responsible for creating the conditions for our release and for our suffering. It takes wisdom and dedication to do this.

Buddha taught that salvation should be achieved by us and not dependent on others.

Mind is the best healer

Buddhism holds that the mind creates the outside world. This is true for our health as well as our body. Many Buddhists combine mantras, meditations, prayers, and medicines to heal themselves and others.

Books and Teachings are essential

Great mentors are important so we can become less ignorant. Reading books is as important as listening to great scholars. Listening to and reading high quality material is one of the most important things you can do in your life.

The Purpose of Life

Life does not have an inherent meaning. It exists by itself. It exists in itself, however, because all people want happiness and to be free from suffering.

You can't believe anything without thinking

Buddhism encourages people to verify everything they read or hear to determine if it is correct.

It is wrong to believe anything. It doesn't matter where it was read or who it was said, as long as it is consistent with our common sense and reason.

## Chapter 15: Tolerance

Tolerance is another important aspect of Buddhism. Buddhism emphasizes tolerance. It teaches you to be tolerant of others in everyday life, to be tolerant when faced by difficulties, and to forgive when it is wrong.

Tolerance is a principle that many prominent Buddhists believe Buddha taught. Tolerance is the key to happiness and true bliss. Hardships come, hardships go. The human spirit is what remains. Tolerance means to see through the obstacles and not lose sight of your ultimate goal.

This aspect of Buddhism is even more important because it overlaps with the message that Buddhism and other religions teach about peace and love. Tolerance would lead to us all tearing each others apart, instead of sitting down together in an assembly with representatives from every corner.

Tolerance is about facing challenges and looking at them in the eyes. Tolerance is about not losing sight of the possibility and believing in oneself. Consider a situation where you find yourself in financial difficulty. Your future prospects look bleak and your relationship with your partner are in danger. You feel like there is no escape from such a situation. Tolerance means acknowledging the problems and finding solutions without losing heart. Tolerance does not require looking for shortcuts or feeling desperate to make things work better. Acceptance, perseverance and a sense peace will get you back on track.

Tolerance can be applied to all situations, not just hardships. It is normal to feel anger if someone wronged you, such as someone who has cheated. Buddhism forbids you from pursuing someone who is full of revenge. You are required to be patient and to learn to accept the situation. This may not be an easy thing to do but it will help you to let go.

It is tolerance not only for one another but also for other religions. One of the most important aspects of Buddhism is their inability to be labeled as "Hindus", "Muslims", or "Christians." They are only concerned with their own teaching.

It is possible to look back on history and not find one instance of a war fought for Buddhism. This is how this religion appears. It doesn't try to convert or preach. It does not hold any promotional events, but tries to reach people. It is unlikely that you will see any Buddhists on social media promoting their religion. This tells us that Buddhism is all about happiness. It's about being happy with what you have. It is not about converting or getting more people to do more. It's all about each individual being a Buddhist.

There are many ways to be open-minded in your daily life. You can forgive people for wrongdoings or accept different views in a heated debate. This could be the most valuable lesson we ever learn if we are open to learning. It is possible to achieve ultimate success by not losing patience and striving for improvement.

# Chapter 16: The Fundamental Beliefs of Buddhism

Buddhism teaches Buddhists how to think for their own purposes. There are many teachings and practices that Buddhism is practiced in different cultures. There are core beliefs that can be considered to represent most Buddhists, if they are not already.

-Buddha is Not a God: Buddha was an ordinary man and never desired to be considered anything other than that. His teachings do not have any set rules and are not the only way to find wisdom in the world. Buddha said that his teachings should not be viewed as a set of rules or the only wisdom in the world. Buddha isn't the only one who has been Enlightened. Many others have done so, and many more will in the future. Buddha was not the first to spread Buddhism. Some believe that Buddha wasn't the first person to achieve Enlightenment. He was only the first to share this knowledge. The claim that Buddha was the first to attain Enlightenment cannot be proven or disproved. It is, however, not important.

-Do not believe anything without thinking: Buddhism encourages its followers question everything they hear or read. It encourages people examine things to determine if they are true according to their common sense and reason. These included the Buddhists' own teachings.

-Gods and Deities are Cultural: Buddhism does not teach atheism, pantheism, or any other stance regarding gods and deities. Depending on which culture is most influential, some Buddhism schools do not have any gods while others have many. Buddhism believes that Gods are the creation of a specific time and culture. Buddha believed it was more important to end your suffering than to continue endless discussions about God's true nature or other unanswerable questions.

The Purpose of Life: Buddhism teaches us that life has no intrinsic meaning. Life exists by itself. Because all living beings desire happiness and to end suffering, one could say that life has only one purpose: to end suffering.

This life affects the Afterlife: Buddhism says that we will reincarnate in another life after this one. This and previous lives will have consequences. To enter Nirvana as a Buddhist, one must educate himself and meditate to avoid the cycle of rebirth. This book will discuss the term Nirvana. Nirvana, the ultimate goal of Buddhism, is it. It is a transcendent state of being free from suffering, desire, or any sense of self. Nirvana means that the person has escaped the effects of karma, and is freed from the cycle between death and rebirth. This is not enlightenment. To attain enlightenment, you must be awakened and aware of the reality that exists but which most people don't see.

-Educating Oneself is Important: Buddhism teaches us that listening to great teachers and reading about them is one of our most important actions in our lives.

Meditation Is The Key: Meditation can be used to calm your mind and examine your beliefs and nature. Meditation is done while you are sitting down. Mindfulness is when you do this while doing other activities. Meditation is the only way to enlightenment. Later in Chapter 11, Meditation and Buddhism, we will discuss meditation more.

-Healing starts in the mind: Buddhists use mantras, meditation, and prayers to heal themselves. The mind is responsible for all aspects of the body, including health and external conditions. Therefore, they believe the mind should be treated.

Buddhism holds that each person is responsible for his own suffering and freedom. It takes personal wisdom and commitment. Others cannot make us meditate or study.

The Body is Precious: Long life is very rare, so it is important to stop suffering. It is important to stay healthy and all life that is reborn as a human being is considered very precious.

-A Spiritual community is essential: While there are no requirements in Buddhism for you to attend a meditation class or temple, it is beneficial to your motivation, understanding, and sense of purpose.

-The Nature Of Reality is Interconnected: Also known as "emptiness", Buddhists believe that everything in the universe can be connected to all other things. Every object, concept, being and being is connected to its cause and the environment around it.

-Doing good is better: Buddhism encourages doing good deeds and not only following rules. Buddhists believe in karma, which states that what we do for others will affect us. There are five precepts in life that can be used to guide you towards positive outcomes. We will cover them further in Chapter Nine: The Five Precepts.

-Compassion: Understanding and wisdom can be extended to compassion. Wisdom is the ability to gain compassion. Understanding becomes stronger when we have compassion.

-Strive for Balance: Buddha taught that moderation was the key to all things. You should not be too strict with yourself or others.

It's never too late to start: This is a common Buddhist belief. You will suffer less if you are less ignorant.

# Chapter 17: Different Schools Of Buddhism

"I won't look at another bowl with the intent of finding fault but rather as an opportunity to learn." - Buddha

Buddhism is over two thousand fifty-five hundred years old, so it's not surprising that it splits into a few institutional or doctrinal sections.

However, the most widely accepted method of describing these schools is the three doctrinal school, specifically "The Ancient Teachings (Theravada)," "The Great Vehicle (Mahayana) and "The Diamond Way (Vajrayana). "The Ancient Teachings" is Theravada. The Pali term theravada means "school of the senior ministers", and it can be traced back to the Sthaviriya, a notable among the oldest Buddhist schools.

It has existed since the fourth century, approximately a thousand years after First

Buddha's death. It is the doctrinal branch of Buddhism that follows the Pali Canon.

This collection of Buddhist writings is the core of Buddhist instruction, practice, and customs. Theravada originated in Southeast Asia and South Asia, especially in countries like Cambodia, Laos and Thailand, Sri Lanka and Myanmar.

The practice is also performed in China, Bangladesh and Malaysia, Vietnam, Vietnam, Nepal, and other countries, but only by a few groups. The "instructing and exam" is Theravada's center for education. This clarifies that the expert's experiences, basic thinking, as well as the functional use of learning, should be the source of wisdom.

This does not mean that one should ignore the advice of the wise throughout their otherworldly journey. Perhaps both the wisdom from one's experiences and the lessons learned by the wise should be taken into consideration.

The Theravada Path begins with "Adapting," then "Practice," and finally, "Attainment." Learning The understanding of "The Three Marks of Existence", is the foundation of the Pali Canon. This standard collection of traditional Theravadan Buddhist sacred texts, is called learning.

The wisdom of "The Four Noble Truths" then follows it. Theravada also clarifies the concept of Defilements (kilesas). These "lethal mental state" can be described as "lethal mental conditions" that prevent a Buddhist from being able to practice Samadhi (extreme focus).

These Defilements may be temporary in that they melt away and wax away but Theravadins explain that they can still cause harm to others as well. According to Theravada lessons there are five types of Defilement called the "Five Hindernisses".

Each one can be presented in three levels: medium, coarse, and unpretentious. The "Five Hindrances" include: Sensory Desire, (kamacchanda), This is the need or thirst that includes five senses: taste, smell and touch. Malevolence (vyapada). Any belief that is related to feelings of hatred, contempt, contempt, or intensity falls under this Hindrance.

Sloth-torpor is a dull personality and slow body that prevents one from thinking deeply and leads to discouragement, torpidity, and even worse, a dull personality.

Fretfulness stress (uddhaccakukkucca). Thoughts and feelings that cause stress or uneasiness hinder the brain's ability to achieve the state of calm that is easily achieved through reflection. Question (vicikiccha). One's lack of trust is what prevents one from achieving Samadhi. Theravada suggests that it is important to think about conquering the Five Hindernisses with the ultimate goal of entering the state of exceptional fixation.

Theravadins also stress that ignorance (avijja), is the primary driver of a man's ability to transform the Five Hindrances into potentialities. Mindfulness and understanding the Five Hindrances are the first steps towards conquering them. Theravada also teaches the concept of Cause and Effect (Pratityasamutpada).

The Pali Canon divides two types of Causes: encouraging (pacca) and root (hetu). The Effect is created when these two causes are interconnected. The Effect must be eliminated from all sides in order to disappear.

Yearning Buddhists need to be reminded of the Truth every once in a while, however. Rehearse Theravada suggests that you practice the Seven Stages of Purification ("Visuddhimagga") with a specific goal to end Suffering and attain Enlightenment.

These are the Seven Stages of Purification: Purification through Conduct Purification in Mind Purification in View Purification of Overcoming Doubt. Purification by Knowledge of Path and Not Path.

Purification by Vision and Knowledge of the Course of Practical.

Information about rise and fall Knowledge on Contemplation Of Dissolution Knowledge Knowledge of Appearance As Terror Knowledge Knowledge of contemplation Of Danger Knowledge Knowledge of Contemplation Of Dispassion Knowledge Knowledge of Desire For Deliverance Knowledge Knowledge of Equanimity About Formations Purification Knowledge Knowledge and Vision Change of lineage Stream-champ is the path to Enlightenment in Theravada. It is understood as a positive method of reinforcing your brain.

To be more specific, contemplation can be divided into vipassana and samatha. Samatha means to be "adroit," to be "quiet", or to "picture and accomplish."

This type of reflection is meant to increase one's ability to focus. Once you have achieved Samatha idealization, you will be able to practice Vipassana contemplation.

This is because Vipassana means "conceptual comprehension" (or "knowledge). This kind of reflection allows the mind to transcend obliviousness in order to see the truth. According to Theravada Buddhism you must always eliminate Defilements in order to attain Enlightenment. While the act of care monitors the Defilements, they should be removed through consistent and reliable thoughtfulness with the goal of recognizing their Causes.

Each Defilement should be linked to more than one time until the Buddhist succeeds in removing them all. Fulfillment Theravadins believe that there are four levels to knowledge and that steady practice can help one attain the insight necessary to become distinctly Enlightened.

These are the "unremarkables" and "supramundane." Once you have seen each of the Three Marks, you will be able to attain "ordinary" intelligence. You will gain a greater understanding of each one, which will enable you to achieve "supramundane" insight.

Presently, "supramundane", or "shrewdness," has four levels. They are all grouped under the Seventh stage of (Purification of Knowledge, Vision). These are: Stream victor (Sotapanna). The "Stream-champ", or "Stream enterer", is the person who has "commonplace" shrewdness after evacuating the first three chains.

These are the False Self-see, Skeptical Doubt and Clinging to Rites & Rituals. The false belief that what is exacerbated will last is called Self-view. This makes the person possessive of the Self, as indicated by the use of "mine", "me," and "I"), which prevents one from attaining Enlightenment.

Wary Doubt refers to a lack of trust in the Buddha, his teachings, or his group. This prevents the being from becoming able to learn through experience. Sticking to Rituals and Rites is the false belief that one can be unadulterated by only performing rituals (counting droning, making offerings, and giving up), or depending on a god to provide non-causal conveyance.

Once-Returner, Sakadagami. After removing the first three chains, the "Stream-victor", becomes an "Once Returner". In other words, he reduces the shackles that cause scorn and desire. Non-Returner, (Anagami). The "Non Returner" is someone who has permanently removed the five lower shackles which fasten creatures to the ordinary world, particularly one that they encounter with their faculties.

One Who is Worthy (Arahants). Once you attain Enlightenment, you will transform into the "Person Who Is Worthy" or "Aharants". This means you have freed yourself from all defilement. It also signifies that you are done with your obliviousness, want and sticking.

Mahayana Buddhism is the most universal of all three schools. Mahayana may have originated in India.

It spread quickly to Southeast, South and East Asia at that time, particularly in Bhutan, Bangladesh and China.

Mahayana Buddhism is seen as the path of competition to be followed, with the ultimate goal of attaining Perfect Enlightenment. It is also known as the "Incomparable vehicle" to illumination.

The Parable of the Burning House Mahayanists love to tell the story of three vehicles (yana), that characterize the Sutrayana Schools of Buddhism. It's the Parable of the Burning House. Legend has it that the First Buddha taught it to Shariputra.

The Buddha told the story this way: "Shariputra let's say there is a particular town in a certain place where there was an a wealthy man. He was very old at the time, but his fortune was so great that it could never be stopped.

He owned large fields and many manors and had an incredible number of hirelings. He lived in a chateau that was so vast, one could still enter it and leave it by a single door.

This house was home to many people, probably five hundred. The chateau was old and crumbling. Its columns were rotting. Its dividers were dilapidating. And its roof was unstable and disintegrating. The fire quickly broke out and consumed every room.

The well-off man's children, twenty to thirty years old, were still in the house unaware of the looming disaster. The well-off man was immediately dreadful when he saw the fire and thought, "I should have the ability to escape through that door." However, my children are still inside the house and having a good time.

They must be near the fire, and they will soon experience much pain and endurance. It may not be possible for them to escape, as their brains are not equipped to handle such a situation. The affluent man said, "I am solid." He then proceeded to say, "I can cover them with a blanket and place them on a chair so that I can lift them up and take them out of the house to security." He continued to consider, however, that there was only one entry to the house and it wasn't wide enough or sufficiently long to pass through.

My children are still active and don't realize how dangerous the fire can be. They get so involved in their games that they may become too addicted to them. They will most likely be smoldering from the fire. They should be made aware of my motives for being so fearful. The house is burning now. I should quickly get them out of the way and save them! After making these considerations, the well-off man quickly entered the house and began to shout for his children: "You should immediately turn out!"

His children were still too fascinated by their entertainments, and not interested in listening to him speak. They didn't feel the fear and anxiety that their father was experiencing, so they were able to flee the house without much effort.

Even more disappointing is that they didn't understand what a fire was, how dangerous it was, or how it was consuming their home. Instead, they just played and looked at their father without following his advice. The rich man began to think.

If we don't get out of this house quickly, my children and me will be undoubtedly burned. It is time to find a sensible way to help my children escape from this burning house. The wealthy man was able to identify the toys that each child likes and what they enjoy.

He then realized that his most beloved toys were rare and difficult to find. If you aren't carrying them around with you right now, it will be a mistake. Your bull trucks, deer trucks and goat trucks are all available outside my entryway. They're ready to be used.

It is your responsibility to get out of the house and have fun with them. I will give you whatever toy you need. The children felt compelled to run as fast as possible out of the burning house after hearing the words of their father about the open door.

After the children had passed through the entrance, the wealthy man gave them each a huge gem-encrusted carriage pulled by a white bull. After the Buddha had finished his story, he inquired if the rich man was guilty of deceiving his children. Shariputra's response was: "No, he wasn't, World-Honored One.

The wealthy man made the effort to save his children from being burned and killed in the home. He is not guilty of lying. This is because the children still had a toy or a likeness of it.

Even more important was his ability to use his intuition to save them from the flames. The Buddha said, "The Buddha resembles the father," which is the "father" of the world, and that the children resemble those who are introduced to an old, rotting, smoldering house, the triple world.

"Shariputra, the wealthy man, attracted his children from the smoldering home by using the three different types of carriages. He gave his children the huge bejeweled carriage which is both the most comfortable and secure carriage ever made. The well-off man wasn't guilty of lying, however.

The Buddha does the same, and he isn't lying. To educate the three vehicles and to direct the living creatures, he then uses the Great Vehicle to save them all. Why? It's because the Buddha is a great power, intelligence, and dauntless. This is also the reason for the location where the Dharma is kept. He is able to give every living thing the Dharma the Great Vehicle.

But not all living things have the ability to achieve it. Shariputra, you must understand why the Buddhas return to earth. They then show the three Buddha vehicles by making these distinctions. Apart from the Parable of the Burning House and a substantial part of the Mahayana Buddhist lessons are a free arrangement of the various lessons that may exist at the same time.

These lessons are based on the fact that all animals can experience freedom from pain. Another idea is that everyone is capable of attaining Enlightenment in a single lifetime. However, this is only if one is committed to taking care of the Buddha, the mantras and custom discourse and understanding the Mahayana sutras.

The majority of Mahayana specialists place stock in mysterious bodhisattvas – Buddhists who deservingly receive nirvana but defer it to teach others. Bodhisattva Bodhisattva is the central figure in Mahayana Buddhism.

The Mahayanists point out that it is too tight. This makes it difficult to attain Enlightenment and be free from agony. This is because it doesn't inspire one to help other conscious creatures become free from suffering. Bodhisattvas are those who are awakened and find a way of doing so.

They are fit to achieve nirvana. However, they value the importance of helping others find it. Bodhisattvas are well-known for their goal to achieve the Trikaya (or turning out to have boundlessly shrewd Buddha), when they can. This allows them to be of greater benefit to other conscious creatures.

You must be able to identify yourself as an abnormal Bodhisattva and have prajna, exceptional intelligence, and a hugely empathic personality.

Mahayanists also believe in the existence of many Buddhas and Bodhisattvas who reside in different domains. Mahayana Buddha is depicted as being transcendent and otherworldly.

As a rule, The Buddha Principle is Mahayana Buddhism's Buddha Principle. It refers to "a heavenly nature which is the fundament to aware creatures to become Buddhas."

Mayanists believe that every being has a hidden, but not indestructible connection that will lead them to the Enlightenment. This connection, which is deep within each conscious being and consists of the "pith and the self" as well as deathlessness, is also believed to be secure.

Mahayanists cannot be combined under one Buddhist school. Perhaps Mahayana is more of an umbrella that can cover a wide range of schools. The Bodhisattva is generally acknowledged as the perfect.

"The Diamond Way" or Vajrayana? If you are familiar with Tibetan Buddhism, you will be happy to know that Vajrayana is the general name for it. This Pali word literally means "the Diamond Way" (or "the Thunderbolt Way") in Pali. Ancient texts also mention Vajrayana being used as a perspective for one of the three vehicles in the Parable of the Burning

House. The other two vehicles are the Mahayana and Theravada.

These antiquated writings about Vajrayana can be found between the third to the twelfth centuries of years in India. However, the word itself is found in eighth-century writings. The Vajrayana convention, which is similar to Mahayana in its goal, seeks the Bodhisattva status.

This shows they are distinct from Theravada. Theravada has, as you probably know, the goal of edification and not aiming to become a Buddha. Vajrayana hone follows the Buddha Principle in an indistinguishable manner from the Mahayana.

Be that as it might, their custom is what makes them distinctive, particularly the Vajrayana Tibet passing custom or the phowa. Phowa refers to a reflection practice which shows "the act or cognizant biting down the dust".

This is done at the Buddhist's Snapshot of Death. Vajrayana Buddhists believe that this will allow the Buddhist's awareness to pass out through their highest point and then it will ascend into The Pure Land, the divine domain where the Bodhisattva lives.

The Phowa allows the Buddhist to keep a strategic distance of the common encounters that can occur after one has thrown the bucket. In order to attain extreme Truth, Vajrayana Buddhists also perform tantric systems.

These methods can be essential or cutting-edge, as the Mahamudra demonstrates. Mahamudra is a term that means "extraordinary image". A propelled expert in Vajrayana Buddhism may use this method to feel reality with peace and uncommon knowledge.

Tantra Techniques

There are many ways to recognize antiquated Tantra writings. The Fourfold division was first identified by the Sarma or New Translation schools in Vajrayana.

As per them, Buddhist religious writing has four classifications, in particular: Action Tantra (Kriyayoga), which concentrates on the significance of custom, Performance Tantra (Charyayoga), which concentrates on the significance of contemplation, Yoga Tantra (Yogatantra), and Highest Yoga Tantra (Annuttarayogatantra), which has three sub-divisions: "mother," "father," and "non-double."

The Nyingma, or the Ancient Translation School, uses another type of division. This includes the Outer Tantras and the Annuttarayogatantra, which are divided into three Inner Tantras. Kriyayoga Charyayoga/Upayoga and Yogatantra are the Three Outer Tantras. The Three Inner Tantras include: Mahayoga and Anuyoga. These Tantra strategies are both mind-boggling and easy to understand.

If you're interested in learning more, these terms can be used to conduct additional research. To gain a deeper understanding and practice these techniques, a Vajrayana instructor is required.

Annuttarayoga Tantras The Annuttarayoga Tantras depict two phases of customary Vajrayana. These practices can be best seen through Buddhist teachers who are guaranteed to do so. To give you an idea of the two stages of these practices, here are some examples: Completion Stage and Generation Stage.

It is a known fact that the Generation Stage represents the underlying stage. This is when one practices divinity yoga. This refers to the ability to recognize oneself with the representations of meditational Buddha.

A guided contemplation would be offered to the wannabe to help him or her focus on becoming "one" with God. The competitor would imagine the "Four Purities" as the center of the stage, while he or she organizes the era.

It is important to note that Vajrayana's Four Purities are exclusive and what distinguishes it from other schools of Buddhism. The Four Purities include:

Seeking one's body and surroundings as the pure land of the divinity; Perceiving oneself as the raptured god; Performing one's activities solely for the benefit of others - philanthropy.

The competitor will then be able to move on to the Completion Stage after the Generation arrangement. The competitor can choose to use either the Path of Method (thabs lam) or the Path of Liberation during this stage. The wannabe can pick the Path of Method (thabslam) to learn Kundalini Yoga. This yoga takes advantage of the body's vitality framework, especially the chakras, and the vitality levels.

Kundalini Yoga draws one's "wind vitality", or "wind energy", towards the heart chakra. It will then be broken down. Once this is done, the competitor will be able to change both his mental and physical faculties. If the applicant chooses the Path of Liberation, he will hone Mindfulness.

This reflection would allow the novice to discover the truths about innate Emptiness. This concludes our definitive talk on the Three Schools of Buddhism.

Each Buddhist should be familiar with the divisions and set aside time to focus on each one. It is essential to remain curious and adaptable, especially when you are embarking on an otherworldly journey to find yourself and the path that will lead to true Enlightenment.

I hope that this particular part has provided insight into a substantial portion of your questions regarding the many learning and practices of Buddhism. We will continue to explore the idea of suffering in the next part.

## Chapter 18: Precept of Right Speech

Right speech is directly related to the importance and value of living.

Teachings of Buddha

Buddha believed that vileness of speech leads to vileness inside.

Action Some people believe that venting is better than waiting.

Use abusive and negative language to get out your inner turmoil. Talking in a

This is the new "cool": A non-respectful, degrading way of being human is acceptable. This is

Because people believe that speaking foul is more acceptable, it is considered acceptable

Rather than acting in bad faith

They don't realize that speaking foul is also an act.

vileness. It is common to observe that tongue disagreements increase.

It can then spiral into physical problems. Often people start by

Using foul language against one another is a form of disagreement verbally.

Language against language can lead to a host of problems.

A person starts a fight with another person by hitting them.

Even if it doesn't happen, vile language can cause so much harm. It is.

You can cause harm to others in ways that are worse than any physical injury. What is it?

If bullying isn't wrong speech, People will tell one another they are

You are ugly, fat, stupid, and many other negative things. These are just a few examples of such words

Sometimes, a knife can penetrate deeper than any sword.

Right speech in Buddhism is defined as the avoidance or occurrence of:

1. 1.

2. Exaggeration

3. Forked Tongue

4. Filthy Tongue

Lying

It is the most widespread and common vice. It is a very common vice.

It would not be wrong to suggest that it is the root cause of the problem.

Complicit in all other vices of the world. There is no other evil in the world

Can sustain itself without lying. It is possible to sustain itself without the help of lying.

person steal if he didn't lie? No! He would defend himself!

He then spreads false stories. This simple vice is now abandoned

This can help you get rid of bad habits.

Exaggeration

Exaggeration is a common practice among many people around the globe.

Without any regret. They exaggerate the virtues of one thing, while

Understating the positive qualities of another. Exaggeration is the only way to describe.

Celebrity culture and personality worship are two reasons. Exaggeration

is also closely linked to a fault when developing the right perspective. One is a.

One is more likely to see things as they are, even if one cannot perceive their basic, raw nature.

They exaggerate their capabilities. This can lead to many problems.

Particularly when you find the real deal.

It disappointed me. As with everything else, this causes undue suffering.

Forked Tongue

A forked tongue is one that says one thing to another.

you do to someone else. This practice can often lead to problems.

A rift is a disagreement between two people. It is the equivalent of planting hate seeds.

It causes both suffering and dislike. It is because of this that it

It is recommended that disciples of Buddha adopt correct speech.

Avoid the forked tongue.

Filthy Tongue

I've already spoken about filthy tongue. It is the truth.

That is what comes to mind when someone first hears "right speech".

Buddha said that vile intentions can lead to a vile mouth.

Turning around leads to vile acts. Pure intentions are the same as pure intentions.

The action of speaking with your tongue means that it is peaceful and will not cause any harm.

Suffering for anyone.

# Chapter 19: The Buddhist Search for Afterlife

We have discovered many great Buddhist teachings that can help us achieve mindfulness and alleviation from suffering. But what about when we die? What is the Buddhist idea of an afterlife? Many Buddhists will tell that this was a straightforward teaching by Buddha. He clearly stated that heaven and hell are realms we create.

The power of our minds is what creates heavenly or hellish conditions. The happy, enlightened mind attains Nirvana (Heaven), while the destructive, negative mind sinks to the depths of hell. The Buddhist idea of an afterlife is divided into two mental states, but that's not all. Buddhism claims that there are specific "planes" of existence dedicated to Heavenly or Hellish states of consciousness.

To be more precise, Buddhism's teachings place all living things into 31 distinct categories and states. These categories include concepts of Heaven and Hell, as well as unique states that the animal kingdom has and for other spirits and demons who are suffering in many different ways.

Buddhism doesn't discount the existence demonic and twisted souls called "discarnate" beings. These beings are called "discarnate" because they are not able to have a physical body and are between death and rebirth. They live on different planes. According to Buddhist beliefs, hell is a place that holds all negative thoughts or feelings.

Six other realms of positive exist alongside the repository of the negative. Six different plans exist for heavenly existence. Buddhism draws a lot from Hinduism to explain how to reach these happy realms. This is something you must be able do on your own. It cannot be influenced by any religious practices or divine beings.

Many Buddhist belief systems now explore reincarnation. This is because if you fail to attain the right amount Karma during this lifetime and your enlightenment fails, you can go back to try again. It's like a cosmic video game that shouts at you "Game Over" and then asks you to play again. Then, after you have put your karmic coins back into the slot, you return to level one to start all over again.

This belief is at the heart of Buddhist Karma. Buddhists believe that reincarnation is not due to supernatural intervention. It is just the natural process of our bodies returning to the Earth. Reincarnation is when our consciousness lacks something we need. According to Buddhism, this happens when we are aware of it. It is almost as if we reach Heaven's gate only to find that the keys have been lost and must return to Earth in order to retrieve them. This is what gives rise to reincarnation.

Buddhism explains that it is a universal and natural law of consciousness that causes us to keep going back until we attain the right amount of Karma. Buddhism teaches that we can only take what we bring with us to the other side of the world. The attainment of "The Brahma", a person who lives in an almost eternal state of bliss and calm, is the highest level of Heaven.

This state is only for those who were skilled in meditation during their entire lives on Earth. The Brahma state is a state in which a being lives in pure consciousness and has no physical body. It is said to be almost like a star floating through space for billions upon billions of years. Brahma beings can be blissfully aware of all things and are in harmony with the universe.

Strangely, my own vivid dreams of being in this state were very vivid. I vividly remember dreaming that one night I was a gigantic sun floating in outer space. I was a huge ball of hydrogen gas, and yet I was fully aware in this state. All of my worries and fears about humanity had left me. I was content to radiate my love and warmth for all eternity.

Although it sounds absurd, this was my real experience in the dream. I can only imagine how the Buddhist concept that all-knowing universal Brahma consciousness is similar to this feeling. Buddhism's main principle regarding the afterlife is that each person must take responsibility for their thoughts and actions in this world.

Many people believe that Buddhism doesn't believe we are punished for what we do. Buddhism, unlike Christianity and other religions, rejects the notion of forgiveness for sins. It eliminates all possibility of pardoning karmic sins. Buddhism teaches that all of us must face the consequences of any negative actions or feelings we may have experienced in our lives. Buddhist beliefs state that there is no easy escape and no escape from our iniquity.

Even though we must face the negative feelings we create, that doesn't mean that we will be punished forever. This simply means we must take the time and get rid of these negative feelings. True to Buddhist tradition, we must face these feelings head-on. Only then can we move on to the next step towards Nirvana. Buddhist teachings state that there is no escape from the negative effects of our actions and that the Karma we create on this planet will be with us until the afterlife.

Buddhism's most important concept is the belief that no outside force can forgive us our sins. Instead, it is the power within ourselves. Buddhism says that only you can forgive our negative thoughts. It is our responsibility to remove any negativity we have created.

Many Buddhists see the call to do good deeds as a way of atoning for past mistakes. They can build enough good Karma to compensate for their bad Karma. This belief is common in the Eastern world. According to the Christian tradition, "good works" do not suffice to get into Heaven. Many Buddhists believe they can just grease the pearly gates enough to make up the past mistakes.

Buddhism is based on the belief that, no matter how bad their past karma was, if enough good karma is generated, then the bad karma can be overcome and forgotten. This allows the person to be in a "good mental state" when they die.

This brings us to the main question about the Buddhist concept for the afterlife. What is the Buddhist view of reincarnation? According to Buddhism, all living things are capable of reincarnating themselves. Every life form in the universe, including an amoeba and sentient beings like humanity, has a spark of life, a life force within them. That energy doesn't die if they get rid of their physical shells. It must go somewhere.

Buddhism says that all living things on Earth have some residual, unreasonable anger. Buddhists believe it is this anger and indignation which keeps all living things on this plane of existence. They are unable to let go of the anger and resentment they feel at their death and they always end up back here!

The Buddhist considers the state of perfect Nirvana, or the "Heaven", the unambiguous end of self and the freedom from the cycle between death and rebirth to be the true state. This is also known as "deathless peace", the ultimate goal for Buddhism. It involves the ending of self and the ending of rebirth. The reintegration with all that is oneness in the universe, resulting in death.

## Chapter 20: Meditation Preparation

Meditation is an integral part of the Buddhist way to live. Meditation is much more than just thinking about nothing. Many people who have never tried meditation have a wrong idea of what it is all about. Meditation is a way to quieten the mind and allow the subconscious mind to function in the background, unimpeded by thoughts from the conscious. Our daily lives are filled with too many stimuli. We are bombarded with information every day. Meditation can help to balance that, but it also does more. Meditation allows you to think clearly and be more productive, as well as to feel closer to your spirituality. Step 6 is about getting ready to meditate and mentally preparing.

Preparing a place where you can meditate is a necessary step in meditation preparation. Meditation is not something you can do if you don't meditate regularly. Meditation takes practice and discipline, which is often lacking in our modern world. This space will help you keep your promise that you will meditate. You will see colorful paintings of flowers in Buddhist temples around the world. There will also be Buddhist statues. However, meditation is not worship. It is believed that these paintings and statues are a source for inspiration that people can use to meditate and gain the most from meditation.

You might decorate the area you use to meditate. Maybe there are small statues that can make the space more inspiring. You can even incorporate post cards about Buddhist events. In my meditation area, I have a stool to meditate, an altar with inspirational memorabilia, and incense sticks as well as candles. Candles are more useful on dark days, when my spirits need to lift a bit. A yoga mat and singing bowl are also my belongings. The Tibetan bowls are used by many people to get the correct pitch for meditation chanting. Although you don't have to chant, a beginner can use the singing bowls to get the right pitch.

You will find that you spend more time choosing meditation as you become more skilled. You can expect to meditate daily for between 20 and 30 minutes, depending on how advanced you are. A place where you can relax and enjoy fresh air in your home is essential. It's important to choose somewhere that's not too hot or too cold.

You will become more proficient at meditation and be able use inspiring places like beaches at sunset and sunrise or other places you find meaningful that bring you closer to nature. These would be too distracting in the beginning stages. Your meditation space should be somewhere that you can relax and is away from distractions.

Maybe you have a cushion that you want to use for meditation. You might even have a meditation outfit. However, this should not be restrictive as it could distract.

Talk to everyone in your home about your desire to meditate. It should be quiet and without interruptions. If that means your family has to turn down the music or TV in their bedrooms, they should respect your need for this time. This is a brief time period and you should not insist on being disturbed by their noise.

Preparing for meditation is very important. You will likely be disturbed if you meditate without having a place to call your own. This will make the meditation useless. To ensure that you have a successful meditation experience, it is important to find people who will respect your decision to meditate on a daily basis. It is important to pick a time when you can relax and switch off, not just eat.

Turn off your phone during meditation. If clocks are distracting, move them to another area during your meditation session. Many people meditate enjoy the ticking clock. They use it to count down. Others find it distracting. It is important to adapt the environment to your meditation style and your individual sensibilities.

# Chapter 21: Is it a religion or philosophy?

There are many arguments and debates about Buddhism as a religion or philosophy. Some argue that it's a philosophy, as first Buddhism doesn't have an image or concept of God. His followers follow him on the basis of experiential teachings and beliefs. They do not rely on God or any supernatural beings. It is said that Buddhism can only be understood if you practice it. It is only through practice that one can fully experience its transformative power. Buddhism that is merely a collection of ideas and concepts is not Buddhism. Because Buddhism has its doctrine, it is also a philosophy that can be used by others.

Buddhism was not an intellectual religion, but was based on imagination and the image of liberation. Commentators have noted that the Buddhist traditions are rich in metaphysical beliefs and that their practices and rituals are rooted in complex worldviews. It is a question that many commentators are asking whether Buddhist practices can be extracted from this environment, without compromising their identity. The calming of passions is what Buddhism is all about. It is the calming that helps one see the truth. While there are many issues and arguments, no one can definitively say whether Buddhism is a philosophy of religion. It cannot be a religion even if it has no image of God. Even if it is based on experiential teachings, the teachings cannot be considered a philosophy. It is more important to see how people respond to it. It is how they react to it and how it affects their lives. Although it can be difficult for some, the end result will be well worth it if your heart is pure.

## Conclusion

Although Buddhism is a religion that dates back hundreds of years and a school that teaches the same principles, we can still use it in our everyday lives. It may be a good idea to bring back old views to help you feel satisfied and happy again, despite all the suffering and turmoil in modern society.

Many people believe Buddhism is a fad religion that doesn't have a place in our everyday lives. But you might find this the answer you need when you feel anxious, depressed or unhappy in your life. This guidebook has taken the time to look at the fundamental tenets of Buddhism and discussed how they can be applied in your everyday life.

Although you may not feel the need to convert to Buddhism, this book will help you make a deeper connection to Buddhism. It will also help you understand how ancient teachings can be applied to your own life to alleviate anxiety and cravings.

www.ingramcontent.com/pod-product-compliance
Lightning Source LLC
Chambersburg PA
CBHW071836080526
44589CB00012B/1012